THE SPANIARDS

HOW THEY LIVE AND WORK

Volumes in the series:

The Spaniards

HOW THEY LIVE AND WORK

Michael Perceval

FREDERICK A. PRAEGER, *Publishers*
New York . Washington

BOOKS THAT MATTER

Published in the United States of America in 1969
by Frederick A. Praeger, Inc., Publishers
111 Fourth Avenue, New York, N.Y. 10003

Library of Congress Catalog Card Number : 74-84857

Printed in Great Britain

Contents

List of Illustrations

(Photographs by courtesy of: Ministry of Information and Tourism, 'La Actualidad Española' and others).

To my mother

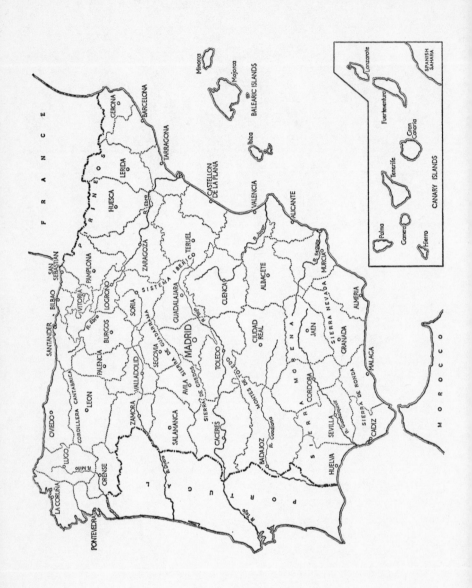

Foreword

In this book, Spain has been compared in many instances with the United States and Great Britain, in other instances with France and Italy, to which the country is closer in the economic development league. The result of such comparisons is to point up, unfairly, the distance which Spain still has to travel along the road of development. It is therefore most important in these introductory words to emphasise that, while the following chapters necessarily reveal elements of organisation still to be reformed and brought into line with the industrialised nations of the West, the real miracle is that Spain can now in fact be compared with these nations. Not so many years ago such a comparison would have been impossible. Over the last decade, however, profiting from political stability, Spain has sprinted from being a nineteenth century society to being a twentieth century one and this, rather than the areas in shadow still awaiting development and organisation, is the truth, the real news from contemporary Spain.

The tables and graphics, by Jose Luis Romero of the DATA research firm, show that progress has been dramatic. It has not yet wholly reached the sphere of statistics, so no reader should be unduly alarmed at any facts and figures he may meet elsewhere in apparent conflict with the ones given here. Nowhere is the enchanting variety of the Spanish experience more visible than in the realm of statistics and in the basic information and documents from which statistics are built. The Spanish tradition in organisations both private and public has been one of non-communication in these spheres, and the information freeze takes time to melt though it is indeed melting.

I have benefited from the important work of investigation in the sociological field by the FOESSA report (No. 1) Fomento de Estudios Sociales y de Sociologia Aplicada) prepared by the DATA team under Amando de Miguel (Columbia University) and supervised by Professor Juan J. Linz of Yale. Invaluable for chapters 4 and 6 is the work of pungent condensation by Professor Ramon Tamames in his *Introduccion a la economia española* (Alianza Editorial, Madrid).

Madrid 1968

I

Introducing Spain

SPAIN is never happy unless she is being misunderstood by other countries. These do their best to oblige by swallowing the many 'black legends' which paint her as cruel, narrow-minded and inquisitorial, and which have almost invariably been circulated by Spaniards in exile. And throughout history, exile for Spaniards has been as normal as whooping-cough for others. The visitor can therefore dismiss any event which might confirm the Spaniards as cruel, narrow-minded or inquisitorial; it is just 'black legend.'

'Africa begins at the Pyrenees,' said Napoleon, yet it was his minor war across the mountains allied to the British naval blockade and the impossible Russian campaign, which unravelled his continental empire. In British history books the Peninsular War, strategically similar to the Allied North African Campaign in World War Two, was a triumph for doughty English soldiery and the generalship of Wellington, always outnumbered, always successful, despite rather than thanks to the Spanish ally, whose army and *prima donna* commanders were the most incompetent in Europe. For the Spanish schoolboy, on the other hand, the War of Independence (the same war) was a stirring victory for Spanish arms, decided by the obscure battle of Bailen and the siege of Saragossa. As it happens, both interpretations are wrong. The war was decided by the ruthless Spanish *guerrilla* bands, spurred by national sentiment, which never allowed the French to concentrate their superior forces to drive Wellington into the sea.

This case of basic misunderstanding typifies a thousand. But if Spain is eternally misunderstood, it is because she starts by misunderstanding herself. As the philosopher Ortega y Gasset put it, ' We don't know what is the matter with us, and *that* is what is the matter with us.' Though not for lack of introspection; imperial and economic decline over the centuries was matched by a state of national hypochondria, of constant abstract debate on ills and remedies conducted in cafés and salons in terms of *topicos* or clichés whereby blame could be laid on the crafty British or the aggressive Americans, the landowners or the Anarchists, the Spanish Catholic Church or the Protestants of Europe, even (the most plausible culprit) the weather. But never on self. History records no case of a Spaniard who confessed to being in the wrong. The very language has no phrase for ' being wrong,' and at most will allow its user to ' make a mistake.'

So for centuries, practical solutions were neglected for utopias lovingly outlined. Perhaps it is part of their strong Arab heritage, a lack of objective mental rigour, but Spaniards flee from realities into rhetoric at the least excuse. Even their statistics are as much a rhetorical as a scientific exercise. Hamlet-like, they think for long periods without acting, only to act in the end without thinking. And yet in *personal* relations, Spaniards possess an unblinkered, intuitive, sardonic realism that runs rings around naïve Northerners. The divorce in Spain between appearance and reality, the official and the actual, which will appear throughout this study reflects the split, the antagonism between the individual and society, between ego and other egos.

On one occasion at least, self-knowledge was offered to Spaniards, when their idealistic-realistic dilemma was symbolised by a mind of decisive wisdom and compassion. Who could call Cervantes a writer of fiction when he gave Spain her schizophrenic national character of Don Quixote/Sancho Panza?

Can the eighteen million foreigners who now visit Spain in a single year come only for the sedation of sun and wine, cheap and abundant though they are? Can they ignore the quality of life around them, its character moulded by extremes of summer heat and winter cold? Unlike Anglo-Saxon society, elaborated

from a thousand compromises and the common sense which is
community sense, Spanish society is a shell of jealous orthodoxy
constraining the molten lava of anarchy. The individual is para-
mount, his dignity, his honour, his magnanimity. The greater the
gap between the Spaniard's concept of his dignity and the objective facts of Spain's power, the greater the Spaniard's sensitivity
to criticism. Criticism, like everything else in Spain, is taken
personally, and ridicule for the Spaniard is like prussic acid on
raw flesh.

A history of civil wars has shown the tragic side of Spain's
'stoicism up to the point of explosion' in civic affairs, but the
positive side of the Spaniard's war against society is a spontaneity
and naturalness of emotion and affection which cherishes children where Anglo-Saxon inhibitions lead to animal worship at
best and child murder at worst.

Economic backwardness, now being remedied at speed, means
that in many ways, Spain is still a 19th century society. Nostalgia
for this on the part of outsiders would be an insult to the poverty
of peasants in depressed Andalucia and Extremadura. On the
other hand, we should not ignore the patriarchal virtues of the
countryside, the courtesy, the kindliness now bound to succumb to
traffic poisoning and commercialism. A society in transition, Spain
is still an atoll of humanity in the ocean of Western standard-
isation, sturdily human when everyone else attempts to be merely
humane. The disadvantages are glaring injustices and the anti-
functional mentality which spawns a bureaucracy scripted
by Kafka from a story by Gogol. But the administration,
State or Church, can work rapid wonders when its heart is
touched.

Spain is a country to live in rather than to work in, and what
the businessman can accomplish in a single morning in London
or New York may take a week in Madrid, where the boss is
always out having coffee, and nobody else can take a message, or
knows about the matter in question, or wants to know. But the
visitor to Spain who rages that 'things do not work' misses the
logic of his own remark. Naturally, *things* do not work. It is
people who either work or fail to work. Spain's chain of mole-

cules is hooked up on the basis of people, and any attempt to bulldoze through on the basis of mere things is doomed to frustration, like trying to push a one-way swing door the other way.

The force of inertia, the most powerful in Spanish administration, ensures that matters of the simplest routine can perform themselves (as Spaniards describe it) by themselves. But anything two millimetres outside routine falls into uncharted jungle, and only intense and pathetic dramatisation of the case will induce a clerk (an *authority*), to venture into this jungle to your rescue. When his automatically defensive reaction piles up the difficulties you must display perseverance and *simpatia* (agreeableness) which lifts the matter on to the personal level—where nothing is impossible. At this level, rules can be shattered to allow human values to flourish. But woe betide the man or woman who takes for granted that *things* will work, simply because they pay for

———

'The Lady of Elche,' one of the peninsula's earliest and loveliest inhabitants, now at the Prado Gallery, Madrid.

Last citadel of Moorish Spain, the Alhambra at Granada, russet ramparts protecting filigree stucco decoration and delicate patios inside.

them. Though tactical rage may help at the right moment, un-
pleasantness in general merely releases the clerk from any obligation to help, and converts the most massive organisation,
commercial, banking or official, into so many hundred individuals with no feeling of corporate responsibility at all.

So it is not just Africa which begins at the Pyrenees, but something rather more complex. It is not clear air turbulence that
your aircraft hits over these mountains, but a subtle, unnoticed,
trailing wisp of the Fourth Dimension, time travel, which fails
to register on the pilot's instruments but nevertheless plays havoc
with the time-scale. Men are four years younger when they land
in Spain, and women, I am sorry to say, are four years older.
And as nature abhors a time-vacuum, all activities are expanded
by a process of Parkinson-like constant creation, to fill the many,
many hours available.

———

Columbus aloft in Madrid.

Cortes aloft at Medellin, in Extremadura. Discoverer of the
New World and conqueror of Mexico respectively.

B

3

How the Country is Run

SINCE the end of the Civil War, Spain has been run from El Pardo palace outside Madrid, residence of the Head of State, General Franco, in whom all civil and military powers are vested. This was established in a Law of 1938 and has been only slightly modified since. Spain has no full written constitution, but a series of fundamental documents allowing considerable flexibility. There is a Parliament, the Cortes, sitting in Madrid in specialised committees and less frequent plenary sessions, for the moderate amendment and approval of Bills passed down from the Cabinet. The latter is the real Parliament, and the real debate is on alternate Fridays around the Cabinet table at El Pardo, chaired for long meetings by General Franco. The Government is no authoritarian monolith, but a coalition of the right-wing forces triumphant in the Civil War, enlivened over the past decade by younger and efficient technocrat ministers, several of them members or associates of the Catholic laymen's movement, the Opus Dei. These have encouraged a movement towards Europe and out of isolation.

By September 1968 there had been eight Franco Cabinets in thirty years, with seventy-six ministers in all, no change being more than partial, as Franco builds his Governments as Jerez blends its sherries, adding new to old but preserving the flavour in the barrel. Since the end of World War Two there have been Christian Democrat ministers in spheres like Foreign Affairs and Education, and military ministers who of course represent their services and watch over internal order. The Falange (Spanish

Fascist) ministers have become fewer with time. The Falange itself has been diluted for a long time into the National Movement, whose creation is the ' organic ' democracy of a corporative State, the *Sindicatos*, social welfare organisations etc. The more radical elements in their platform—land reform, nationalisation of banks and public utilities—have never progressed very far.

Having defeated the Socialist and Anarchist mass movements and the small but effective Communists in a long and savage war, the victors were unlikely to allow re-emergence of their enemies for another round to please the victors of the World War. All opposition political activity is firmly squashed therefore, even if greater freedom of speech is now permitted to the intellectuals.

The régime actively groups the military, the National Movement (Falangist-staffed), most Monarchists, right-wing Christian Democrats, moderate conservatives in general, and in theory the Carlists (mainly Navarran Jacobite-style traditionalists). The opposition ranges from dissident groups of the above, through several shades of left-wing Christian Democrats and Socialists, to Basque and Catalan Nationalists and the extreme varieties of Anarchist and Communist. Denied the right to organise, to participate in government, or to oppose it legally, the embryo parties are no threat to the régime, which enjoys the support of the broad spectrum of the people, who are living better than ever before in Spanish history, and desire firm government (of whichever wing) as a bulwark against chaos, so familiar over the past century and a half. On the other hand, should power pass to the opposition by default, as happened in 1931 with the Republic, it will of course fall into hands without practical experience guided by spirits very naturally bent on revenge.

Political orientation or identification of Ministers in Spanish Governments (1938-1962)

Falange, without previous political allegiances	8
Falange, with previous allegiance to CEDA (Catholic Centre-Right Party)	5
Technocrat, with Falangist orientation	4
Falange total	17
Traditionalists (Carlists or similar)	3
Monarchists	2
Member of Primo de Rivera régime	3
Christian Democrat (Centre-Right)	3
Opus Dei members	3
Non-political experts, civil servants, technocrats	10
Centre-Right total	24
Military with Falangist orientation	3
„ „ Traditionalist orientation	1
„ „ Catholic party links (C.D., Opus Dei)	2
„ „ CEDA links during Republic	2
„ „ Primo de Rivera régime	2
„ „ with no special orientation	16
Military total	26
total	67

Source: Juan J. Linz 'An authoritarian régime: Spain,' in *Cleavages, Ideologies and Party Systems. Contributions to Comparative Political Sociology* (ed E. Allardt and Y. Littunen, Helsinki: Transactions of the Westermarck Society, 1964, pp 291–341). (Data taken from Spanish version)
(Note: Falangist and military contribution was heaviest evidently in the war years.)

The régime's concern is thus to ensure that power does not pass elsewhere. The question is how long the coalition engineered by General Franco can survive its creator, for Franquism is a pragmatic, characteristically personalist balance, deriving from the fact that in Spain, unlike the Germany and Italy of the thirties, the General Staff defeated the politicians.

Factors working against the unchanged continuation are the pro- and anti-Monarchist divisions within the coalition; the points at which economic efficiency and partnership with Europe clash with authoritarian organisation; rising standards of education and living to provide a basis for stable party democracy, and the emergence of a younger generation (65 per cent of Spaniards are post-Civil War) fully in touch with developments outside the frontiers and impatient with the dogma and liturgy of the thirties.

Factors working in favour of relatively stable transition are the need to preserve economic advances and tourism income, and a species of constitution and succession mechanism prepared by General Franco in 1966 and approved then in referendum. This *Ley Organica del Estado* shows a pro-Monarchist inclination, but leaves most options firmly open. A 1947 referendum had already declared the country to be a monarchy, but Spain, unique in a world of kings without kingdoms, was still in 1968 a kingdom without a king.

POLITICAL THEORY AND ORGANISATION

Any future king installed under the terms of the *Ley Organica* would have to promise observance of the main features of the régime, which include the 1938 Labour Charter (due for reform soon) creating the vertical *Sindicatos* or State trade unions linking labour and management in obligatory membership; also the Spaniards' Charter, brought out in 1945 with a series of rights and their practical limitations, and the Principles of the National Movement which emerged in 1958. These enshrine concepts of geographical unity (anti-separatist) and the rôle of the armed forces in maintaining that unity and internal order. Many principles are self-evidently desirable, such as stress on links with Hispano-America and the improvement of health, mining and irrigation. Others, such as the pledge to implement Catholic doctrine in Spanish legislation, are subject to broad interpretation in that Catholic doctrine upholds the right to associate, found political parties and go on strike, whereas Spanish legislation does not. The principles expound that political representation in Spain is via 'natural' entities—family, municipality and *sindicato*—these groupings replacing voluntary affiliation to an ideology.

The *Ley Organica* brought an innovation in the shape of direct suffrage to elect 'family representation' members of the Cortes to a fifth of the seats. The remainder are still filled directly by the Head of State, evolved by indirect elections within the various local authorities, learned and professional associations, the *Sindicatos* and the National Movement. The Movement's National Council of just over a hundred seats is something of an embryo Senate. The Cabinet in full also sits in the Cortes, bringing the total seats to 564, though several members occupy two seats, so that seating outnumbers incumbents. With the independence of Equatorial Guinea in October 1968, the departure of ten Guineans presumably reduces the total to 554. As the monthly salary of a Cortes member is about £18 ($43) other jobs have to be maintained full-time; 377 of these were provided by the State in 1968, in civil service or 'autonomous' organisations.

The Organic Law allows for a future Prime Minister picking his own Cabinet, but the document, while extremely detailed in describing the mechanism of political development, is prudently vague about the when of it. The political organisation of Spain, taking it with gross over-simplification, is a pyramid building up from the grass-roots of family, municipality and *sindicato,* through the Cortes to the seventeen-man Council of the Realm and the three-man Council of Regency, with power residing, as is to be expected, in the topmost stages of the pyramid. There is one more body mentioned in the Organic Law and in numerous speeches as guarantor of the system—the Defence Junta of the

top military commanders—and the efficacy of this no Spaniard
doubts.

The Spanish Cabinet Minister is an extremely powerful figure,
ruling his department in considerable independence of his col-
leagues for an average of about five years (though some last
ten or more), depending always on the decision of General
Franco. Hardly ever does a minister go from one department to
another. At the time of writing, the departments are :

Presidency of the Government (Premier or Vice-Premier's Bureau,
    also containing Planning Minister and staff)
Foreign Affairs
Justice
Army
Navy
Air (also handling civil aviation)
Finance
Industry
Agriculture
Education and Science
Public Works (including transport)
Interior (including health and post office)
Labour
Information and Tourism (also running TV and National Radio)
Housing
Commerce (also running the merchant marine)
National Movement (its Minister also head of *Sindicatos*)

The top jobs in Foreign Affairs and the military departments
are held by career men (diplomats and soldiers respectively), but
the remaining ministries have under-secretaries (14), directors
general of various sections (89), other top posts (182) and sub-
directors general (234) who are chosen personally by the minister
in question as political nominees. They leave office with their

patron and must thus retain links with private enterprise meanwhile, even though many have civil service titles which they never
lose, irrespective of their employment. Ministries with most political jobs on offer are Finance (77) and National Movement (155,
including the heads of 30 different *sindicatos* and perhaps 40 of
the 50 civil governors of provinces, named in conjunction with
the Ministry of the Interior). Ministers earn just under £6,000 a
year ($14,400), and directors general about 60 per cent of this.

Spain does not appear to know how many civil servants are
actually employed, estimates ranging from 0.8 per cent to 1.8
per cent of the population, not counting the 130,000 local
government officials. Statistics are hindered by the numbers on
contract, those holding full status but not currently acting as
civil servants, the military in civil ministries and civilians in
military, the inclusion or non-inclusion of primary teachers and
armed forces regulars, and of course the myriad ' autonomous '
organisations. These range from the State Railways to the football pools, via the massive Social Security Institute and Nuclear
Energy Board. Not only are the staff and income of these unknown, but also the actual number of these organisations, though
they may total around 350.

The lower ranks of the civil service are badly paid and have
no *sindicato* to defend them in relations with their employers.
Most of them need two or three jobs to make ends meet, though
the main sufferer tends to be the citizen who has to deal with
them. However, there are *gestorias*, professional agencies which,
for a fee, handle the citizen's contacts with the bureaucracy. The
top ranks, on the other hand, may earn £6,000, while a variety
of incentives may double this amount.

The top corps of civil servants (there are perhaps 195 different
corps, but a dozen only form the *élite*) are authentic mandarins
—State advocates, diplomats, Council of State advocates, university professors, fiscal inspectors, road engineers etc, and are
often simultaneously retained by private enterprise. They provide about 80 per cent of the ministers, under-secretaries and
directors general as well as a large proportion of Cortes membership. Career success for a Spaniard therefore lies in official Spain

rather than industrial or business Spain, ensuring a life-long sinecure job with high pay (in the mandarin corps) and extensive perks. The obstacle is the ferocious competitive examination known as the *oposicion*, designed to substitute objective intellectual criteria for nepotism in candidate selection. The *oposicion* may mean the sacrifice of six years of youth in post-university study, but triumph in this is triumph in love as well as life, for the hand of a girl of good family is gained simultaneously with the *oposicion*.

LOCAL GOVERNMENT

Spain is divided into fifty provinces for administrative convenience, some rich, many poor. Each has a civil governor taking orders from the Madrid Ministry of the Interior and matched by a military governor. A *Diputacion Provincial* can offer advice, but not take decisions. Each province is divided into *municipios*, municipalities currently numbering around nine thousand. Those with more than ten thousand inhabitants have an *alcalde* or mayor appointed by the Minister of the Interior, while smaller entities have their mayor named by the civil governor. The mayor is aided in his deliberations by a town council composed of the *sindicato*, family representative and associations thirds of the Spanish political system.

As in every other aspect of Spanish life, local government is on the brink of a thorough-going reform, taking into account the population shift from country to cities, which has left nearly thirty-seven per cent of municipalities with less than five hundred inhabitants, and over seventy-five per cent with less than two thousand. Four thousand municipalities have annual incomes of less than £1,250 ($3,000) and may have difficulty in paying their clerks, not to mention firemen and rubbish collectors. Enthusiasm for employment has dwindled, and local administration clerks are still battling for conditions of equality with the staff of the State Administration.

As economic development draws rural Spain into a swifter-paced life, and regional development poles are set up for industrialisation, so the provincial system is under increasing fire as a relic of French-influenced over-centralisation, with all-powerful but dilatory Madrid ruling provincial bodies too small and artificially demarcated to have will, wealth or character of their own. Only Navarre retains a fair measure of autonomy in raising and spending money. Meanwhile, more commentators are coming to advocate a rational but not selfish regionalism, based on the old natural kingdoms which fused to create Spain—roughly speaking, Galicia, Asturias, Leon, Old and New Castile, the Basque Country and Navarre, Extremadura, Aragon, Catalonia, Valencia, Murcia, Andalucia, the Canary and Balearic Islands. However, behind the Madrid centralising tradition is the fear of regionalism leading to separatism and good old Spanish anarchy in administration.

Some regionalism exists in military, hydrographic and other demarcations, which do not however coincide either with each other or with the historic regions, so that a province like Basque Guipuzcoa comes under Valladolid for education, Pamplona for judicial purposes, Burgos from the military point of view, El Ferrol from the naval, Oviedo for hydraulics, Saragossa for the Civil Guard and Bilbao for the security police. Co-ordination is not a Spanish forte.

Local government has had to wait its turn, but there is every reason to expect reforms in this sphere now that streamlining has started in the Central Administration. The hardest thing for a bureaucracy is to improve itself, but a new approach can be observed in Public Works, in Information and Tourism, to name but two departments, where a functional spirit has been imbued from the top, and the rôle of the bureaucracy is seen as one of doing rather than just being. Results are now being obtained in proportion to the size of the machine. While all red tape and contact with the bureaucracy at lower level is still devoutly to be avoided to preserve the citizen's sanity, the difference between the Spanish Administration today and in earlier years is so striking that it amounts to nothing less than a small revolution.

THE LEGAL SYSTEM

' Spanish Justice ' sends an automatic but largely unnecessary shiver of alarm up and down the Anglo-Saxon spine. Unless they bluster and insult, foreigners, bringers of tourist currency, normally receive favourably mild treatment. A bail bond secured at the same time as green card international car insurance saves the visiting motorist from gaol after an accident except in cases of gross negligence. The real disadvantage of Spanish law is not lack of objectivity (in cases other than political), but antiquated courts and organisation, and complex birdcages of laws supplementing or abrogating each other to the confusion of client and lawyer alike. As the law, like most Spanish organisation, is imitated from French models, a magistrate of instruction is appointed in criminal cases to prepare a lengthy dossier as a basis of both defence and prosecution cases. That this legal stalagmite eventually demonstrates his innocence is limited solace to a someone who has spent two years in gaol waiting for his case to be heard.

An example of this was the celebrated methylated spirits case heard in December 1967, where the dossier on the group priming cheap liquor with spirits (killing fifty-one and blinding many more), took 13,000 pages and four years to prepare. In the three weeks of the actual trial, three French tearaways shot up a Madrid bank, were caught, tried, sentenced, and sentence commuted—all in the space of a fortnight. This was feasible solely because crimes with firearms come before summary military courts martial. While offering speed, the rôle of military justice in certain civilian or criminal cases is perhaps the major anomaly in the Spanish system. Surprisingly, this intrusion is not the creation of the present régime, but dates from the first decades of this century, when the military felt themselves at a disadvantage. As a result, the clash of civilian with soldier, private car with military, etc, brings the civilian up before a court martial, not vice versa. It also offers the peculiar spectacle of the military trials of journalists for publishing helpful suggestions on military service or, as in one case in Las Palmas, simply for a poem in favour of peace.

Spain's penal system is full of good intentions, offset by the unwholesomeness of some prisons and the appalling food (expected to be supplemented out of the prisoner's pocket). On the other hand, stiff sentences are never served in full, thanks to frequent amnesties, time-off for days worked, and use of conditional liberty. No trades unions interfere with useful work, and skills are taught, bringing tobacco and wine money in acceptable amounts. Short sentences for first offenders rarely involve actual physical imprisonment, so that Spain has one of the world's lowest prison population rates, just under 12,000 in 1968 for nearly thirty-three million inhabitants. Half of these were serving sentences and the other half awaiting trial. Officially-admitted numbers of political prisoners fluctuate between one and two hundred, and unofficial estimates range around the thousand mark. Political offences range from membership of the Communist Party to membership of the freemasons, illegal propaganda, demonstrations, illegal association (gatherings of over twenty persons without Ministry of Interior permission) and the like. These are now tried by special Public Order Courts, but not so long ago came under military jurisdiction. While this subject arouses fierce condemnation of Spain abroad, and hinders association with the Common Market, the majority of the political prisoners at any given moment will probably be inside for questioning or cooling their heels for short periods at moments of tension.

The organisation of the legal system is the responsibility of the Ministry of Justice, while the law itself is codified, French-style, into Civil and Penal Codes, with their almost as important implementing codes of procedure, as well as a largely out of date Mercantile Code. The decisions of the Supreme Court form a body of precedent interpreting the clauses of the codes. Passing swiftly over the municipal and area *juzgados* or petty courts, we find criminal proceedings start at district courts of instruction and first instance; where an instructing magistrate drawing up the dossier finds a prima facie case established, he remits the prisoner, with or without bail, to trial at the provincial court. There is no jury system, but the prisoner will have a bench of from three to five judges to face at the provincial court, and if he appeals to the Supreme Court's Criminal Division, five to seven justices.

Civil cases in Spain are as slow and costly as anywhere else, but can often be solved at a court of first instance, though appeal carries them to an intermediary territorial court and eventually to the Supreme Court. Many cases are settled out of court in conciliation meetings. Judges, at all save the lowest levels, are civil servants of the Ministry of Justice, and so are the *fiscales* or public prosecutors. The judiciary is a career open to those over twenty-one and possessing a law degree, and is subject to an *oposicion* or competitive examination. Then comes judicial training and promotion by strict seniority until the presidency of a Supreme Court Division comes in sight, when other criteria come into play. The divisions are Civil, Criminal, Public Order, Administrative Disputes and Labour. Administrative Disputes handles cases of the citizen challenging the State and its bureaucracy, while Labour (run by the Ministry of Labour) is a swift, simple and equitable service handling worker-employer disputes which have not yielded to conciliation within the *Sindicatos* arbitration mechanism.

The police are legally bound to hand over their prisoners to the judiciary within seventy-two hours of arrest, but prisoners cannot consult with their lawyers until after questioning by the magistrate of instruction. There is no real equivalent in Spain to the British solicitor, for the *procurador* normally has a lower qualification and is a mere manager of court appearance. Most people get into direct contact with the advocate who will prepare their defence and also plead it in court. These advocates are members of provincial Colleges of Advocates, and number about 23,000, about 15,800 of whom actually practise law. Other legal professions are the notaries, who witness deeds and affidavits, some 1,400 in all Spain, winners of stiff *oposiciones*, and 565 registrars of property, who certify deeds relating to property. Both these professions coin money, as vast numbers of documents and deeds are obliged to pass through their hands.

In crime, Spain is still an underdeveloped nation, though juvenile delinquency has arrived hand in hand with moderate affluence, and car stealing is rife. The *quinquis* or tinkers provide a rough but poverty-stricken underworld. Organised crime does not exist, however, partly as the result of heavy policing, whether by the helpful *serenos* or nightwatchmen of the city streets, the rural guards in brown corduroy, the blue-uniformed municipal police, mostly concerned with enforcing petty regulations, the white-helmeted traffic police, and the more formidable forces run by the Ministry of the Interior. Its Security Department at the Puerta del Sol controls the small but active *Brigada Social* or secret police, with a large network of informers, and also the conventional detectives of the *Brigada de Investigacion Criminal*, whose patience, intuition and reliance on their countrymen's inability to keep a secret, give them an extremely high crime solution rate.

The two major corps of nation-wide uniformed police are organised on para-military lines, the urban *Policia Armada* (grey uniform) and *Guardia Civil* (green with capes, black tricorne headgear). The latter are a legendary body of rigidly-disciplined gendarmes with high *esprit de corps*. They move always in pairs, one with rifle, the other with sub-machine-gun (to the alarm of foreign visitors). Incorporating the carabineers or Customs guards, the corps has some 2,000 officers and 53,000 NCOs and guards. It also provides the highway motor patrols. Many people wish it could also tackle city traffic.

The grey security police are possibly no more than 15,000, mainly in the big cities, and highly mobile with Land-Rovers, apart from the many who just stand guard over embassies and public buildings. Their virtually permanent attendance at Madrid University in water-cannon trucks and Land-Rovers earns them the status of honorary students, with the rubber truncheon notably mightier than the pen.

As each ministry can cheerfully issue decrees and orders, the spate of new legislation is appalling, with ten thousand new legal dispositions in three years from 1964 to 1967, plus 2,472 in the latter year alone. At one new item every three and a half hours, according to some calculations, lawyers all over Spain are pressing for total reform of the system. A scheme for this exists, and it would suppress all special courts (except military and ecclesiastic), while the Supreme Court would have only four Divisions (civil, criminal, administrative disputes and labour), with simplification and streamlining in the lower courts. The judiciary would get its own police corps to ensure that the judge's writ in fact runs outside as well as inside his courtroom. Trials would become less formalistic, allowing greater confrontation and cross-examination (influence of Perry Mason, as the more traditional Spanish advocates describe it, acidly).

DEFENCE

Though a régime of military origin, the Spanish State spends comparatively little on the defence budget, estimated at around 2.3 per cent of the national income, or £6 ($14) per capita compared with Britain's £50 ($120). The main expenditure is on administration and wages for the regulars, as American military aid, worth $550 million (£220 million) since 1953, has largely handled the equipment side. American aid and training courses have led to a remarkable smartening and streamlining of the Spanish forces, with the introduction of sophisticated weaponry and concepts.

If we omit the para-military *Guardia Civil* and *Policia Armada*, Spain's land forces come to around 200,000—220,000, of whom a quarter are regular officers and NCOs, the remainder being composed of fifteen-month service conscripts. Some 30,000 of these troops, including the dashing Legion, serve in Spain's African territories of Ceuta, Melilla, Ifni and Sahara, backed by 9,000 in the Canary Islands. Of the 25,000 or so officers, 821 are generals, over half on the reserve or retired. Promotion in the officer corps is according to seniority (ie place on their year's passing-out list at the military academy), so the younger the officer the more certain is his reaching highest rank. Spain and the islands are divided into nine military regions for administration, and into 'immediate attack' and 'territorial defence' forces according to rôle.

The 'immediate attack' force is spearheaded by the Madrid-based 'Brunete' division, an armoured unit with M-47 tanks. A mechanised division is based on Valencia, and a motorised on Seville. The force also has one parachute brigade, one airborne and one armoured cavalry. 'Territorial defence' has six coastal artillery brigades, plus an independent infantry brigade in each region as the nucleus for general mobilisation. There are two mountain divisions and one high mountain brigade in the Pyrenees. Spain also has US Hawk ground-to-air missiles, as well as her own ground-to-ground rockets. US aid has supplied 105 and 155 mm howitzers and 40 mm and 90 mm anti-aircraft guns, in addition to some 1,500 jeeps and trucks and about 500 tanks, M-47s and M-41s. Spain produces her own excellent automatic light weapons (Cetme rifle etc).

Spain has a long naval tradition, and the present-day Navy comprises around 35,000 officers and men (16,000 regulars, 3,500 of them officers), plus 8,000 highly-trained marines. There are 144 admirals (or equivalent ranks in the land-based ancillary

---

Cervantes broods over his creation, Don Quixote and Sancho Panza, idealism and realism as the conflict in the Spanish psyche. Statue in Madrid Plaza de España.

corps), 51 of them retired. The main bases are El Ferrol in Galicia, Cadiz and Cartagena on the Mediterranean coast. The rôle is mainly anti-submarine and escort, and the Americans have supplied several ships while modernising many more of the older Spanish units. At present Spain has the 13,000-ton cruiser *Canarias*, 7 destroyers of 2,080 tons, 14 modernised frigates and 10 older types, 4 submarines (only one fully operational, strange in view of the fact that Spain invented the submarine), 6 corvettes, 25 mine-sweepers, mine-layers, torpedo boats and other ancillary craft, as well as two American-supplied attack transports and the 14,000-ton helicopter carrier *Dedalo*. The Spanish navy is anxious to acquire its own fixed-wing fleet air arm, but has to be content with four flights of helicopters.

The Spanish Air Force has existed as an independent service since 1945. It still flies a number of German World War Two types such as Heinkel light bombers, and possesses Me109s and Ju52s, even if these have long since been relegated to the second line by American aircraft. The extensive radar coverage of the peninsula is now wholly Spanish-operated, and the US bases at Torrejon (Madrid), Moron (Seville) and Saragossa (de-activated), like the Polaris submarine base at Rota, are carefully described as ' joint-bases ' and run as such. The continued

Holy Week procession at Seville; the emotional, expressive religion of Andalucia.

C

American presence is under negotiation once more at the time of writing, with a reported Spanish asking price of $1,000 million in military and other aid to compensate for the increased dangers of Russian nuclear rocketry.

The 40,000-strong Air Force has 15,000 regulars, of whom 4,500 are officers, while the generals number 126, of whom 55 are retired. Apart from the air regions created for administrative and combat coverage purposes, there are functional commands, Material, Transport, Air Defence and Tactical. The Tactical force operates two squadrons of twenty-five F-86 Sabres apiece, as well as two squadrons of Spanish-built Heinkel-111 light bombers, one squadron of T-6 support trainers, and a wing of naval support Grumman Albatrosses. Air Defence has a squadron of F-104G Starfighters at Torrejon, flown successfully by experienced pilots, as well as four squadrons of F-86. The aircraft of Transport Command include DC-3, DC-4 and Spanish Azor types, lately supplemented by Canadian DH Caribou aircraft.

As becomes the land of Juan de la Cierva, inventor of the autogyro, Spain flies several types of helicopter. Moreover, Spanish aircraft factories are now producing the Northrop F-5 ' Freedom Fighter ', a sophisticated multi-purpose fighter. In service very soon will be thirty-six of the single-seater F-5A and thirty-four of the F-5B trainers.

CURRENCY

Spain's unit of currency, the peseta, was a hundred years old in 1968, with an exchange rate of 70 to the dollar and 168 to the pound sterling. Over these hundred years, the peseta has lost 99 per cent of its gold value and prices have risen by 2,256 per cent. Worth 9.5 to the dollar in 1939, the sickly peseta underwent numerous devaluations, until stabilisation in 1959 triggered the economic boom and made it one of the world's hardest currencies, backed by tourist income and reserves around the $1,000 million mark.

Coinage from the peseta upwards includes the silver-coloured *duro* (five pesetas), larger 25, 50 and 100 peseta pieces, the latter with a silver content to encourage hoarding (saving). The old 1, 5, 25 and 50 peseta notes are now rarely seen, and the standard notes are brown 100 peseta, blue 500 and green 1,000, for which nobody ever appears to have change.

NATIONAL ACCOUNTS

Spain has recently adopted the OECD practice of issuing national accounts, and these revealed a rise in the wages and salaries share of the national income from 53.5 per cent in 1965 to 55 per cent in 1966; at the same time property and private business sank from 37.3 to 36.2 per cent, food consumption from 44 to 42.1 per cent, and saving by companies in gross capital formation from 17.7 to 17 per cent. However, the gross national product, at market prices, rose from 1,287,300 million pesetas (£7,700 million, $18,500 million) in 1965 to 1,616,522 million pesetas (£9,600 million, $23,100 million). National income in 1967 was 1,389,352 million pesetas (£8,300 million, $20,000 million). The dollar equivalents are calculated at the rate of 70 pesetas (November 1967 devaluation, which matched the pound's exactly).

THE BUDGET

Spanish budgets are designed to cover two-year periods (1969 repeating 1968), though in fact the extra credits added after the budget's approval normally add 20 per cent over each twelve-month period. The 1968 budget was divided as follows:

	pesetas
Head of State's Department	24,633,000
Council of the Realm	1,920,000
Spanish Cortes	95,962,000

	pesetas
National Council, Political Studies	
Institute and National Movement Bureau	603,310,000
Public Debt	8,222,794,000
Pensions	18,921,919,000
Accounts Tribunal	43,970,000
National Funds	5,352,132,000
Premier's Bureau	8,457,375,000
Foreign Ministry	2,097,915,000
Justice	6,075,915,000
Army	21,141,220,000
Navy	6,851,801,000
Interior	22,833,748,000
Public Works	35,427,831,000
Education and Science	24,705,690,000
Labour	4,316,454,000
Industry	1,824,062,000
Agriculture	11,102,689,000
Air	9,104,220,000
Commerce	7,908,156,000
Information and Tourism	2,727,130,000
Housing	9,428,414,000
Finance	2,289,526,000
Various ministerial expenditures	28,241,214,000
	237,800,000,000

This 1968 figure of 237,800,000,000 pesetas (£1,400 million, $3,400 million) almost exactly triples the 1961 figure, and gives some idea of Spain's economic advance over the period. On the other hand, foreign experts have criticised the excessive expenditure of the public sector as an inflationary factor, not so much the investment as the consumption excess.

TAXATION

Spain's taxation system has been criticised inside and outside the country as rigid, ineffective and inflationary, for two-thirds of the revenue is raised by indirect taxes (paid in many cases equally by rich and poor alike) which in turn raise prices, while only one-third is direct taxation on personal income and wealth which should be the instrument to redistribute wealth in the interests of social justice. Because of almost non-existent income tax and death duties, the money of the great families remains untapped generation after generation, depriving the nation of its benefits and preserving the great estates, the contrasts of riches and poverty, and encouraging the parasitism of the upper classes. On the other hand, the defence by the individual and the clan of wealth against the State is not a purely Spanish feature, but part of the time-honoured Mediterranean and Latin-American tradition of tax evasion. Taking for granted dishonest tax returns, the State must triple its tax pressure to obtain anything at all, which in turn makes false returns essential, or else the individual would be swindling himself instead of the State. However, the matter is not wholly one-sided, for if the individual has tax returns, the State has statistics.

Budget revenue consists of 61,740 million pesetas from direct taxes, 140,450 million from indirect, and other items (rates, transfers, income from property, changes in financial assets and liabilities etc) accounting for the remaining 35,000 or so million. Of the direct taxes, the major items were 14,500 million in personal earnings tax (deducted at source from wages and salaries at 14 per cent) and 17,600 million in company tax. Business men and the liberal professions can find their way successfully around the personal earnings tax, while the company tax is a block sum levied by the Finance Ministry on the various sectors of trade and industry. Despairing of ever learning true earnings and profits when all firms carried twin sets of books, the false ones for sporadic tax inspectors, the Ministry introduced a global assessment in 1957 whereby each sector was set a sum to be raised within itself. In a spirit of pessimistic realism, the burghers were assembled in medieval style and told to raise tribute money. In this case, of course, the burghers merely pass the amount on to the consumer.

Meanwhile, in 1966, income tax in fact accounted for the ludicrous sum of 2,000 million (£12 million, $28 million) or 1.4 per cent of total tax revenue, an amount matched almost exactly by death duties. The alarming feature is that for several years the amount of the State's Equal Opportunities Fund was tied to income tax revenue. (The fund is designed to provide education opportunities for the poor.) Constantly changing income tax patterns, threats, weakening to appeals, followed by amnesties, deprived the tax menace of its credibility, which could only be restored by computers and effective armies of tax-gatherers. However, the December 1967 reforms, if implemented, could indeed remedy this hole in the bottom of the Spanish bucket.

The 1.4 per cent of income tax (against the 20 per cent normal in advanced countries) in the tax total, allied to high Customs tariffs, indicates the survival of underdeveloped structures and mentality in Spain. Income tax did not exist in the country till 1932, and vanished again between 1940 and 1954. The difficulty is to know just what people do earn, as documents are filled in at all stages to conceal rather than reveal. In 1957 the World Bank report assumed 50 per cent tax evasion, but some Spanish experts raise this to 60 or 70 per cent. In 1954 there were but 232 self-confessed peseta millionaires (£6,000, or $14,400 a year) in all Spain, rising to 450 in 1960, dropping to 383 the following year, and actually reaching 1,796 in 1966, 385 of them in Madrid, in a year when the capital sold 600 limousines, each costing over a million pesetas. Several bullfighters earn a million in a single afternoon, not to mention industrialists and landowners and the thousand top civil servants assumed to reach this sum in a year. But of course, in supposedly authoritarian Spain, the State cannot inspect private bank balances.

The 1967 reforms represent a reasonable tax burden, with the contributor liable to income tax from 300,000 (£1,800, $4,240) of earned income (already paying 14 per cent in personal earnings tax), and 200,000 as the lower limit if the income is unearned. The lowest rate of income tax is 18.2 per cent, rising steadily to 61.4 per cent for incomes of 1,600,000 and over (£9,600, $23,000). Conspicuous expenditure was made an additional criterion in assessing taxable wealth (houses, cars, motor launches etc, not to mention number of servants), though this may commit the injustice of supposing that middle-class families can in fact afford the rents they are forced to pay.

The indirect taxes arouse less emotion—customs duty, luxury and sales turnover tax on goods purchased, petrol and tobacco, not forgetting a handsome lump sum from lotteries. The indirect taxes meet the State's needs, but fail in their social purpose of redistribution. According to Professor Fuentes Quintana, Spain's economy and tax system are in a transition stage where the ambitions are fully developed but the fiscal realities underdeveloped. The number of self-supporting peasants make income difficult to tax, but growing industrialisation will force Spain to monetarise more extensively, while increasing direct taxation.

Some critics maintain that the citizen cannot be expected to co-operate honestly with the State unless he can keep an eye on the State's inner workings through a democratically-elected parliament. This, however, is perhaps taking an over-optimistic view both of the efficacy of parliamentary committees and, especially, the innate civic spirit of the Mediterranean man. The examples of France and Italy do not encourage optimism in this respect. Moreover, one suspects that, fundamentally, economic development, civic spirit and democratic organisation are but three aspects of the same phenomenon, and that none can be advanced artificially at the expense of the others. Only in harmonious interaction can the three aspects progress.

POSTSCRIPT

On 22 July 1969, General Franco abruptly summoned the Cortes and proposed Prince Juan Carlos de Borbon, grandson of Alfonso XIII, last King of Spain, as future Head of State with the title of King. The Cortes accepted with enthusiasm; the Prince swore to observe the Fundamental Principles of the Movement, and the Spanish Establishment sighed with relief to think that the régime would very possibly survive after Franco.

3

The Country and the People

SPAIN cannot be understood without reference to the geography and climate of the four or five distinct Spains. The country's narrow frontier with the rest of Europe is 280 miles of abrupt, green Pyrenees. Thereafter the bull's hide of the Iberian Peninsula stretches west and south till a mere eight or so miles across the Straits of Gibraltar gouge the divide between Europe and Africa, Atlantic and Mediterranean. Portugal removes a strip of western coast, leaving Spain with 195,000 square miles as more than sufficient space for her 32,500,000 inhabitants—including the Balearic Islands in the Mediterranean and the Canaries off the West African coast.

The summer visitor thinks of Spain in terms of sun and beaches, but few realise that this is Europe's second most mountainous country, its average 1,950 ft above sea level beaten only by Switzerland. In addition to the Pyrenees, mountains line the northern coast, rising to the snowy Picos de Europa in Asturias. The lofty Sierra Nevada in Andalucia rises to the 11,400 ft of Mulhacen, and there are a dozen impressive ranges, including the Guadarrama mountains north of Madrid which divide the central Castilian plateau (two-fifths of the entire country), into upper and lower, Old Castile and New.

The effect of the mountains is to produce people with strong local and regional loyalties, but only vague loyalty to the nation as a whole. And this is accentuated by the additional barriers of the big river basins formed by the mighty Ebro, draining the north-east down to the Mediterranean, and the Douro and

Tagus flowing west through Portugal to the Atlantic. Schemes are now afoot to drain off water from the Tagus to remedy the drought suffered by Spain's south-east.

The most evident division of Spain is into wet and dry, north and south, as if Europe extended only to the northern regions of Catalonia, the Basque country, Santander, Asturias and Galicia in the far western corner. In these parts winters may be chill but summers are mild, with frequent drizzle, annual rainfall fluctuating between 27 and 59 inches. The results are glowing green countryside, farmsteads on the farm, cows in the meadow, milk and meat inside the people—though the more barren land of Galicia, over-divided into tiny plots, fails to support a large population for all the guile of its Celtic inhabitants. Speaking a soft dialect of Portuguese in the villages, Galicians have Irish-type dark hair and blue eyes, and play bagpipes. When not emigrating to Argentina or German factories, they produce sardonic literature and dominate the Madrid power-structure. General Franco is but one leading Galician. They give nothing away. As an identification test, you may ask Spaniards the time. The Basque will give the correct time, the Catalan will exclaim that he has an appointment in two minutes, the Andalucian will be running half an hour slow, and the Castilian will refuse to carry a watch. The one who pretends that his watch has stopped is the Galician.

The Asturians (we are now moving eastwards from the Galician corner) are a strange lot, with Welsh-type mining valleys and a tendency to use their skill with dynamite in politics as well as the coal-face. Santander is Castile meeting the sea, and the Basque corner is rich in rolling hills, prosperous Swiss-style farmhouses, solid stone buildings in the villages, emancipated women, and brawny pelota-playing, shy, valiant, reliable men. Most narrow valleys have huge factories, and Bilbao is the industrial capital of Spain, with age-old links with Britain. Meanwhile, Basque shepherds mostly seem to emigrate to Texas. The fishermen and navigators are celebrated—Elcano completed Magellan's trip to achieve the first circumnavigation of the globe—and at least six out of the top ten Spanish bankers and industrialists at any time are bound to be Basques.

The Catalans form a corner between Pyrenees and Mediterranean, and their industry (predominance in textiles) is vitiated by individualism which prevents their rivalling the Basques in banking. Their Manx-cat like language, lacking sonorous final syllables, is essentially Provençal, a Mediterranean development of Latin parallel to Castilian, a result of the French warriors who entered Spain to fight the Moors in the Middle Ages. Like the Basques of Bilbao, the Catalans of Barcelona resent the control of Madrid, regarded as the inefficient home of a parasitic bureaucracy. However, these regionalist tendencies may be counteracted today by the increasing industrialisation of Madrid and the influx of Southern peasants to form the labour force in Catalonia and the Basque country. The Catalans, to veer away from economy for the moment, have an innate artistic sensibility; they produced Salvador Dalí and Joan Miró, while they strongly influenced the Malaga-born Picasso. In the works of the art nouveau architect Antonio Gaudí, Barcelona boasts some of the most striking achievements of the turn of the century in Europe.

The Balearic Islands speak a version of Catalan, amid all the English, French, German and Swedish, and so do the people of the Valencia region, with its luxuriant orange groves and paddy-fields. As one writer put it, Valencia is where the Franks of Catalonia met the South and became soft and feminine, just as the Castilians went soft and subtle in their Andalucian blend with the Arabs. To their oranges and succulent rice *paella*, one of Europe's great dishes, the Valencians add an Arab love of bangs to a Phoenician love of fire, and the result is an annual orgy of incendiarism known as the *Fallas*, when countless fireworks are let off and a couple of hundred huge lath and plaster satirical figures go up in flames.

Inland from the Valencian coast is tawny Aragon, once a power in Europe, fertile along the Ebro, incredibly deserted and rocky around Teruel. The notoriously stubborn Aragonese perform the infectiously catchy dance known as the *jota*, and, in the Basilica del Pilar, boast the patron saint of Spain, the Virgin of the Pillar, who handles the distaff side just as Santiago (St James) is the masculine patron.

Castile, with Madrid in the centre, is the land of the castles, the long-disputed no man's land between Christians and Moors. Central geographically, it became dominant politically through a process of absorption inwards, and its language, a romance derivation of Latin, is what we now know as Spanish but which Spaniards always describe as *castellano*. It is understood all over the country, although some Galicians, Catalans and Basques may express themselves more readily in their own vernaculars. On the other hand, many Galicians, Catalans, and especially Basques may speak only Castilian.

As significant as its political predominance, however, is Castile's rôle as dry steppeland, start of the African element in Spain, with burning summers taking over from freezing winters without appreciable autumns or springs, although to be honest, Madrid in October and January can be a miracle of crisp sunshine and stimulating air. From Castile southwards, rainfall may average only twenty inches, far lower than most of Europe and the Northern States of America. And in this ' extreme ' Spain averages deceive, for they disguise months of drought and parched soil followed by brief February deluges which wash away the dusty top-soil, turn dry watercourses into torrents, and then vanish into the ground or the sea after flooding a village or two, leaving nobody any the better off. A major drive on dams, river control and reafforestation is under way, but it will be some time before the engineers can bury dry Spain.

The farmers may not show enthusiasm, but there is much beauty for the traveller in the broad wheatlands of Old Castile, the ochre land and soft contours of New Castile, just as there is surprise when the khaki uniform of summer Spain is replaced by green on the rolling hills outside Cordoba for a few months before this region becomes the summer frying-pan of Spain once more.

Nature, by and large, has dealt Spain an impressive but unprofitable hand, mainly because of inadequate water supplies. There is uneconomical coal in Asturias, and mercury, uranium and pyrites, wolfram also, to mention valuable minerals, while even in classical times Spanish iron and copper, gold and silver were exploited by Greek and Phoenician settlers. But the natural disadvantages of agriculture have been aggravated by man, recklessly felling trees, creating estates either too small or else too large for economic farming. The latter is especially true of Extremadura—a blend of Castile, Portugal and Andalucia—and Andalucia itself, the part of Spain which most foreigners take to be *all* Spain. For Andalucia is the home of whitewashed houses and wrought-iron balconies, raven-haired women with flowers in their hair, horsemen in chaps, bolero-jackets and Cordoban hats, land of guitars and *flamenco*, of song, dance and bull-fighting, of the wines of Jerez and the Seville Fair. Everything, in short, that tourists love and other Spaniards affect to despise.

POPULATION

Andalucia is also the home of grapes and olives, seasonal crops that leave thousands of peasants unemployed for much of the year and hence natural candidates for the twin emigration waves which are a Spanish revolution of deeper importance than any of the more spectacular political commotions the country has suffered in the last century and a half. To emigration must be added the natural population increase of around a million every three years, as 650,000 are born each year and 300,000 die. The result of this at the end of 1968 is approximately 32.5 million Spaniards, a contrast with the barely 20 million of 1910. Modern medicine has redressed the tragedy of the 1936-9 Civil War in which the same nation had to face the casualty lists of both sides, and also lost several hundred thousand refugees to France. This disaster neutralised Spain's advantages in remaining outside both World Wars.

The fact of civil war prevents records from being kept, so statistics are casualties also. It is impossible to say how many Spaniards were killed or executed, and guesses range from about half a million to a largely rhetorical million. However, what we *can* now see is that the birth-rate dropped by 100,000 a year between 1937 and 1942.

Efforts to remedy this once peace was restored produced legislation to encourage large families. Grants per child never reached the point where it was more profitable for breadwinners to stay at home and breed, but the annual prizes for families with seventeen or more children received much publicity. Marriages are fewer now, dropping from 8.8 per thousand in 1956 to 7.2 in 1966, and family sizes are also decreasing, even though family planning does not exist in Spain's rigorously Catholic context. However, health and hygiene excuses evade the official rules, and about 1.5 million packets of birth-control pills are thought to be sold yearly, mainly under doctor's prescription.

Infant mortality in 1900 was the staggering figure of 203 per thousand, contrasting with the 35 per thousand in 1960. The latter figure should be altered to 43 per thousand, however, as infant mortality in Spain refers to children who die under the age of one year but have survived the first twenty-four hours in order to qualify legally as persons. The rate has continued to drop since then, and it is safe to assume figures of about 30 (legal) and 36 or 37 (real). Improved medicine and hygiene has also brought the general death rate down remarkably, from 29 per thousand in 1900 to 8.6 in 1960. Over the same period, life expectancy rose from 33.9 years for men and 35.7 for women to 67.3 for men and 71.9 for women. This bias in favour of the weaker sex, added to the aftermath of war, means a million and a half widows against only half a million widowers.

The number of people in Spain at any time is hard to judge because external migration has sent nearly four million abroad since the turn of the century, if we include the emigrants to European factories, most of whom return after three or four years. But even more dramatic has been the upsetting of old population patterns within Spain, as austerity caused an agrarian crisis in 1959 while industrialisation gathered momentum. Since then at least two to three million peasants have moved to the cities, and 23 out of the 50 provinces have lost population, even though all the provincial capitals, with the sole exception of the museum-city of Toledo, have gained. The shift is towards five areas: Madrid, Bilbao and the northern coast, Barcelona and its satellite towns, and to a far lesser extent Seville in south-western Andalucia and the Canary and Balearic Island tourist boom zones. The greatest loss is from Andalucia and Extremadura, with New Castile, Galicia and Old Castile not far behind.

Madrid and Barcelona have been the main beneficiaries, and one Spaniard in five now lives in these two provinces (five years before, it was only one in eight). At the end of 1967, Barcelona province had almost 3.5 million people, and Madrid about 3.3. By cities, Madrid had a full 3 million in mid-1968, contrasting with the mere 2 million of 1959. At the present rate of increase, the 1980 figure will be 5.5 and the 1995 will be over 11 million. As the capital is virtually unliveable and certainly unparkable in at the end of 1968, the prospect is alarming. The same fearsome trend may be expected in Barcelona, already 2 million strong (more, if all suburbs are included), and the cities between 500,000 and 300,000: Valencia, Seville, Saragossa, Bilbao and Malaga, in that order.

Proportion of inhabitants living in towns of more than 20,000
inhabitants for various countries

Countries	1910 %	1950 %	1960 %	1965 %
United States	31	42	47	—
France	26	33	38	—
Sweden	16	30	44	—
Spain	23	40	46	50
World	9	21	27	—

Sources: Gerald Breese, *Urbanisation in Newly Developing Countries* (Prentice Hall, 1966, p 19).

Institut National de la Statistique et des Etudes Economiques, *Annuaire Statistique de la France* 1966 (Paris 1966, pp 25 and 26).

Instituo Nacional de Estadistica *Anuario estadistico de España* 1966 (Madrid 1966, p 57).

HISTORY

THE famous bull-paintings on the ceiling of the Altamira cave may or may not produce the bull-fever which is one of Spain's most striking characteristics. It depends on whether you believe that the place or the race produced the man. If the latter, Spain's complexity is impressive, for the pre-historic Iberians, probably of North African stock, have been subjected to successive blends like a rare old tea. Phoenicians founded Cadiz, perhaps in 1,100 BC, while the main wave of Celts came through Europe to settle in Galicia (the north-western corner), attracted by the rain, around 600 BC.

The Basques in the Pyrenees and Biscay Coast region are as mysterious in origin as their language; perhaps they were simply there from the start. Greeks and Carthaginians brought the southern coast into Mediterranean civilisation from the fifth century BC onwards, the latter founding Cartagena and Barcelona (for Hamilcar Barca). Rome began her profoundly influential conquest with the difficult capture of Numancia in 218 BC, and then colonised the peninsula most thoroughly. The evidence still before our eyes ranges from the triumphal arches of Tarragona to the magnificent Segovia aqueduct, the Meridda theatre, and the names of camps all over the country, Pamplona (Pompeiopolis) and Leon (from the 7th Legion). As a result, Galicia is full of people named Castro. And not only Galicia, of course.

Salvador de Madariaga, in his classic study 'Spain', declares that the literature of Rome's Silver Age was Spanish in origin, and the names of Seneca, Lucan, Martial and Quintilian would seem to bear this out. Of the Emperors, Spain can claim to have produced the best—Hadrian and Trajan, Theodosius, even Marcus Aurelius by ancestry. On the other hand, the historian Americo Castro derides this identification with Roman Spain as a flight from the reality of modern Spain's racial and cultural debt to Arabs and Jews, the real ancestors. While there may be much self-deception about the Roman inheritance, one nevertheless suspects that place as much as race must affect a people after a few centuries.

A Teutonic element irrupted in the early fifth century AD, with several tribes shattering Roman Spain politically, and eventually evolving the shaky Visigothic kingdom which adopted Christianity but disintegrated instantly at the Arab invasion in 711. And so the Spanish South ceased to be Vandalucia, after that destructive tribe, and became Al-Andalus, a base from which the many different Arab peoples flowed north to the mountains of Asturias and the Pyrenees, threatening the whole of Europe. Despite successive waves of still more pugnacious desert warriors in later centuries, the Arab part of Spain gradually receded as the Christian kingdoms grew bolder. Even so, the civilisation of Cordoba rivalled Baghdad and Damascus, and the gardens and palaces of Seville and Granada grew from the world of the Arabian Nights. The Arabs were the truest heirs of Greece and Rome, and poetry, philosophy, medicine and the sciences flourished centuries ahead of the rest of Europe. For these brilliant but eternally divided people, the Christians of the North must have represented the permanent barbarian threat.

If the Christian Reconquest—eight centuries of it—was a leisurely sort of affair even by Spanish standards, this was be-

———

General Franco addresses the Spanish Cortes. Below him sit the Cabinet, at right angles to the Cortes Members; white jackets denote Falangists (National Movement).

cause entirely new nations were emerging from the fractured remains of the Visigothic kingdom, with Castile and Aragon gradually absorbing most of the western and eastern halves of the peninsula, before thrusting further and further southwards and themselves merging to form modern Spain just before the final act—the conquest of Granada in 1492. Columbus was waiting impatiently in the Christian camp for the fall of the city, for the end of the Middle Ages, as he had a New World up his sleeve.

THE GOLDEN AGE

The long centuries of struggle had paradoxically meant peaceful co-existence of the three religions and races, all fairly well mixed up throughout the country. But with the arrival of the modern era of nationalism and realpolitik, class and race jealousy, first the Jews and then the Arabs were expelled. Their only alternative was to feign conversion to Catholicism, with permanent fear of burning by the Inquisition for backsliding, as this Kafkaesque politico-religious purge mechanism, unrivalled until our own century, got into its stride. And so the traders and bankers, cultivators and craftsmen crossed from Europe to North

---

Madrid's La Paz hospital, built for the social security health scheme.

Traditional Andalucian houses, gleaming with whitewash. Picasso was born at Malaga, just up the coast from this scene at Estepona.

D

Africa, just as French and Spanish, not to mention Jews, have done recently in reverse, from Algeria and Morocco back to Europe, on another swing of the pendulum.

The discovery of the New World was a Castile exclusive; as the financing came from Queen Isabella's jewels, so the rôle of her husband Ferdinand's Aragon, essentially Mediterranean, was neglected. For in the Americas the *conquistadores* had struck gold, Cortes in Mexico, Pizarro in Peru. This gold was redistributed in part by maritime *conquistadores* like Sir Francis Drake, but even that does not reconcile Anglo-Saxons to this episode of history. We find it impossible to forgive the handful of Extremaduran peasants in armour for dealing with their Indians in the early sixteenth century as Anglo-Saxons dealt with black, brown, red and yellow skins in the nineteenth. What the Spaniards destroyed was unique, alas; perhaps what we really resent is their arriving first. Not everything is negative, however, for evangelisation and culture came in the wake of conquest, though the enlightened laws on colonisation drawn up by great jurists at Salamanca and Alcala failed to have much effect on practice across the ocean. Spanish conquest was more than just political; inter-marriage was the norm to produce today's Disunited States of South America.

The sixteenth century was Spain's Golden Age, one of the great moments of human civilisation, with El Greco painting at Toledo, dramatists like Tirso de Molina (inventing the symbolic figure of Don Juan), like Calderon, like the unbelievably prolific Lope de Vega, 500 of whose 1,500 plays have survived. And, of course, Cervantes, wounded at the battle of Lepanto when Don John of Austria, King Philip II's half-brother, defeated the Turk at sea and saved Europe. Philip himself is not over-popular in Britain, and inherited the imperial worries of his great father Charles V rather than his personality and prowess. But Philip did build a wonder of the world in his monastery-palace at El Escorial outside the township of Madrid, just then elevated into capital of the realm. The Escorial was the Pentagon of its day.

The century was brilliant, but decline lay just over the horizon;

Spain had become a world empire ' on which the sun never set ' before she had consolidated as a nation. As well as the English challenge at sea, she was landed with the European wars of religion as champion of the Catholic cause, and with the defence of the Flanders real estate of her new monarchs, the Habsburgs. For a nation which had expelled her financiers and technocrats, a nation ruled by rigid bureaucracy, flooded with gold and silver but failing to turn it into commerce, the strain was too much. The decline was sharp also in matters of art and intellect; after Velazquez in the mid-seventeenth century loss of spiritual energy was almost complete. The Inquisition had effectively cut off oxygen, so the natural sparks which always fly in Spain could no longer produce flame. The Habsburgs degenerated also, and their eighteenth century successors, despite neat, enlightened, typical Bourbon rule, could only disguise, not remedy, Spain's ills.

But if the glory was brief, it was on the heroic scale, with the *tercios* or battalions of pikemen, the panzers of their day, sweeping through Italy and Flanders; Portugal was added for a while, bringing Angola and the Congo; and across the ocean South and Central America, much of what is now the United States— Florida, California, Louisiana (by later arrangement with the French) and much of the southern interior. Nor should we forget the Philippines and the Pacific island chains; Ceylon, Borneo and Sumatra. Some optimists even claim that Australia was named after the Habsburg House of Austria.

THE EIGHTEENTH CENTURY

But the sea was not always the scene of triumphs, and the beginning of the end came with the defeat of the Invincible Armada in 1588, a loss not only of a hundred and sixty ships and thirty thousand men, but of confidence that God could be relied on as admiral of the Spanish fleet—as Philip had assured the landlubber commander, the Duke of Medina Sidonia. The next humiliation at the hands of the English was in 1704, when the War of the Spanish Succession saw England and Holland pushing another Austrian candidate to follow Spain's deceased line of Habsburgs, while the French, who had already done their best to undermine Spain with Turk and German allies, put forward a French claimant. Admiral Rooke, leading an Allied fleet, captured Gibraltar in the name of the Archduke Charles, rightful King of Spain as he thought. When it was the Frenchman who eventually triumphed as Philip V, Rooke transferred the Rock to the Crown of England, no doubt because the Archduke Charles would no longer be needing it. And British it has remained until the time of writing, vital base for an expanding maritime empire, and permanent irritation to the Spaniards, though efforts to regain it have only sporadically taken military form. Like Calais, which eventually reverted to France, so Gibraltar will obviously revert to Spain. The question, accentuated by the Spanish diplomatic and communications-cutting campaign of the 1960s, is when, and how.

The eighteenth century under the Bourbons was an un-Spanish exercise in rational reform, scientific endeavour which centralised the administration excessively and failed to move the depths of Spain. This *ancien régime* collapsed when confronted with Napoleon, and the people's guerrilla war against the occupying forces was fought on the basis of local juntas or groups, reverting to instinctive regionalism. While French troops besieged the Spanish liberals in Cadiz, these were in fact enshrining the original ideals of the French Revolution in their Constitution of 1812. The scene was set for a century of revolutions and military coups as dogmatic reactionaries and dogmatic liberals attained and lost power, the farce twice degenerating into major civil wars, the Carlist Wars of the 1830s and 1870s. Even the 1936-9 Civil War contained many traditional nineteenth century elements alongside its Marxist and Fascist additions.

THE END OF AN EMPIRE

The nineteenth century abroad was as bad for Spain as it was at home, starting with the revolt of the American colonies and

ending with the Spanish–United States war of 1898; the loss of
Cuba, Puerto Rico and the Philippines, last remnants of empire,
being accepted as the nadir of Spanish fortunes. With the loss of
the colonial markets and Spain's stagnation in post-imperial
lassitude, Catalonia and the Basque Country—the only areas
which had caught on to the industrial revolution—gradually
turned their cultural regional feelings into separatist nationalism.
The only compensation for Spain lay in literature, where the
angry young men known as the 'Generation of 1898' were not
content to luxuriate in national hypochondria without seeking
radical solutions, and achieved memorable books at least. The
Basques Unamuno and Baroja, the Galician Valle-Inclan, the
Mediterranean Azorin and the Castilian Ortega y Gasset are the
only Spanish writers to win an audience abroad since Cervantes
—whose 'Don Quixote' was the first warning of Spain's impend-
ing failure in a mercantile world.

Spain was neutral in both World Wars, but the early decades
of this century found the country caught up in a Moroccan campaign. Military disasters in this forced King Alfonso XIII (married to a beautiful granddaughter of Queen Victoria) to accept
the military coup of General Primo de Rivera in 1923. This
dictatorship lasted until early in 1930, but its external progress
and modernisation attempts only masked and accelerated internal
decomposition. When Primo de Rivera fell, Alfonso had run
himself out of ring space, and was forced to abdicate soon
afterwards to avoid (as it happened, to postpone) civil war.

THE CIVIL WAR AND AFTER

The Second Republic (1931-36) started in a climate of optimism but in a deteriorating economic situation; the liberal intellectuals lacked strength to impose their will on either the Right
or the mass movements of the Left. Elections revealed disillusion
with whichever side had most recently been occupying power,
and the sides were largely insincere alliances of groups designed
merely to top the polls on the great day, even if they disintegrated

the next. By 1936 there were 600,000 unemployed, strikes were endemic, and so were street shootings between Left-wing and Falangist gunmen. The recent and alarming examples of the Bolshevik and the Hitler Revolutions were a warning to both class groupings, with annihilation the prospect for the loser. The Spanish Civil War really began with the attempt in 1934 by the Asturian miners to establish a Soviet in their region, a bloody effort suppressed still more bloodily. The next round came with the definitive explosion of all the latent class, religious and regional wars in the July 18 rising of 1936, when Navarran Carlists, much of the army, and the small Falangist party launched what should have been a swift coup but turned into a long war, involving Germany and Italy on the Nationalist side, Russia and to some degree France on the Republican.

And so Spain, after long oblivion, featured again on the world map, in a manner tragic for the inhabitants caught up in the struggle, either from ideological conviction or geographical accident. As a theatre of war which was also theatre of fact, Spain engaged the idealism of young people all over the world, and on the Republican side inevitably, as the people are a more promising symbol than the generals, bishops and bankers on the other. However, as the effect of propaganda dies away, it seems clear that Spain witnessed two simultaneous revolutions, Right and Left, with the Madrid Government a helpless spectator. In Western eyes Nationalist Spain was damned by its totalitarian cast and its Nazi and Fascist allies. Nevertheless, General Franco managed to keep his stricken country out of the World War, enraging Hitler with his stubbornness. In retrospect, the refusal to let German troops cross Spain to Gibraltar, so sealing the mouth of the Mediterranean, weighs heavier than the raucous pro-Axis propaganda with which the Falangists were saturating Spain at the time.

The United Nations boycott of Spain after the World War and the denial of Marshall Aid added a few more years to the economic disaster dating back to 1936, but did not damage the régime. Almost the reverse, it helped the irreconcilables within the borders to feel equally punished by outsiders, and prevented the much-needed arrival of Western ideas other than those of the fallen dictatorships. It was the cold war and the American need for bases in Spain which effectively began the slow liberalisation of the country and its economic recovery from 1953 onwards—though much of the basic structure had already been provided by the Spanish National Institute of Industry and its factories.

General Franco's seventy-sixth birthday in 1968 found him still in power, an apparent miracle in turbulent Spain, and a tribute to a master of pragmatic politics, Fabian in the style of the Roman general who employed inaction, timing, and a great talent for balancing and ruling. If the prosperity achieved in the final part of his reign proves lasting, Spain may desist from her pendulum swings from one extreme to the other. At the time of writing, Spain is moving tentatively from her pro-American position to try a more Gaullist line. The political signposts for internal development point in two opposing directions still: towards the Greece of the Colonels or towards the Italy of subtle democratic balancing acts.

RELIGION

Spain is nominally ninety-nine per cent Catholic, though the actual level of religious practice varies greatly—extremely high in the Basque country and the Pyrenees, extremely low in Andalucia and Extremadura where churches and instruction are scarce. The middle classes attend mass regularly, the urban proletariat hardly at all. Nevertheless, religious questions move Spain deeply, irrespective of the level of practice, and the Catholic Church has long enjoyed cultural domination and social influence on morals and customs (at least in the realms of the Seventh Commandment), interrupted only by occasional bursts of the anticlericalism nurtured by intellectuals and workers.

One period of anti-clericalism began in the 1830s and saw the confiscation of Church properties, in return for which the State has since paid diocesan clergy a small monthly wage.

Participant of the reactionary-versus-liberals battle of the nine-teenth century, the Spanish Church was barred from education by the Second Republic, and the religious question was one of the more important sparks igniting the Civil War, in which some fourteen bishops and six thousand priests, monks, nuns and seminarists were executed or murdered on the Republican side.

Restored to temporal dominance by the Nationalist victory, the Church exercised censorship on books, films and plays, and in some areas banned dancing and forced men bathers into full-length suits. It also harassed the non-Catholic minorities, closed their chapels, impounded their literature. Divorce was absolutely prohibited after its brief appearance under the Second Republic. Today, while the stand on divorce is in no way modified, the more bizarre aspects of Church control over society have diluted to vanishing point, the works of Sartre and other authors danger-ous for the spiritual health of the Spanish flock are sold freely in the bookshops, advanced plays and piquant films abound, advertisements for lingerie appear in the newspapers, and on the beaches the bikini, bringer of tourist currency, goes unmolested— by the police, at least. Thanks to a decade of contact with the West, Spain is no longer run as a seminary, and even the older bishops may realise that there are more Commandments than one.

Part of the trouble has lain in the generation gap between the Spanish bishops, average age sixty-seven, and the clergy, where the old and the young suffer from the lack of a bridge generation to interpret for them. The missing generation was killed or dissuaded from the priesthood in the Civil War. The limited reading and bureaucratic experience of the bishops makes it impossible for them to understand the activity of the young priests among the working classes and their identification with claims for social justice. As well as a political revolution, the Spanish Church requires a managerial revolution to match the great population shift from countryside to cities. At present young priests are stuck, furious, in semi-deserted villages, while there are city slum parishes of over 50,000 people without effective religious contact. Much will have to be changed if the 26,000 secular priests, 25,000 monks and 83,000 nuns (the monks and nuns largely engaged in teaching and nursing) are to play a significant rôle at a time when vocations for the priesthood are declining sharply in any case as a result of the population shift and the smaller size of families.

The non-Catholics number around forty thousand, with Moslems estimated between one and three thousand, including students from Arab countries; Jews are assessed variously at five to eight thousand, mainly in Madrid, Barcelona and the North African enclave cities of Ceuta and Melilla. The Protestants are thought to number between thirty and thirty-five thousand practising members, divided into eight main denominations, with Seventh Day Adventists and Plymouth Brethren among the largest, followed by Baptists and Episcopalians. They claim perhaps a hundred thousand more sympathisers whose adhesion has been prevented by the administrative difficulties which until recently surrounded Protestants (or rather, any non-Catholics wishing to avoid the pattern tailored rigidly for the Catholic majority) in matters of baptism, education, marriage, burial, military service and civil service employment.

By the time that a Religious Liberty Bill was passed in 1967 (Spain is bound by her 1953 Concordat with Rome to implement Catholic teaching in her civil laws, and Vatican Council II endorsed religious liberty as a positive good), the situation for the religious minorities had improved considerably, though still falling far short of the status of the Catholic Church.

THE ROLE OF THE CATHOLIC CHURCH

The rôle of the Catholic Church in Spain, its influence over the civil power, can only be understood in a historical context. Engaged over eight centuries of sporadic conflict in repelling the Moslem invader and driving him out, the Spanish Church acquired a permanent crusade complex, and formed a number of military-religious orders in imitation of the Moslem élites, to act as spearhead in the struggle. Thus politics and religion came to be identified and have not yet been disentangled, unfortunately. However, this capacity for strong reaction in the Spanish religious mentality has created three of the world's most remarkable religious orders: St Dominic Guzman's Dominicans, a reaction against the Albigensian heresy of the late Middle Ages; the Basque St Ignatius Loyola's Jesuit shock troops leading the Counter Reformation, and today Mgr Escriva de Balaguer's association of laymen, the Opus Dei, reacting against the materialist forces of the modern world. It has been pointed out that while Italy produces the mild religious orders, Spain produces the combative ones.

But if Catholicism in Spain remains a potent influence and a perilous detonator of political and emotional reactions, its achievements in the realm of the spirit should not be neglected. The sixteenth century saw a flowering of mysticism in the overwhelming personality of St Teresa of Avila, in the poetry of St John of the Cross, and in several more writers, intellectuals and jurists.

4

How They Live

SPANIARDS are community-livers, apartment-dwellers, and the isolated house with protective gardens hardly exists save in the tourist developments eating up the Mediterranean coast. In the cities everything is four or more storeys high, and the striking new luxury blocks soar to ten or twelve, their flats selling at £12,000 ($28,500) to £48,000 ($115,000), renting at anything up to £250 ($600) a month. Long-established city-dwellers on the other hand may well enjoy virtually unassailable tenure of old flats at absurd, frozen pre-war rents of £2 ($4.80) to £6 ($14) a month. Landlords cannot afford maintenance of such blocks at such rents, and so spend most of their time introducing death-watch beetles into their property, leaving gutters unattended, until such time as the place can be declared a ruin, the tenants evicted, and a spanking new edifice put up with apartments for sale only.

The poor new arrivals to the cities must share insalubrious small homes, put up shanty-towns, and intrigue for a letter of recommendation or similar extra-curricular plug into the system which will enable them to move into one of the mammoth low-rent housing estates on the outskirts. With the usual lack of co-ordination between Spanish authorities, the cities fail to catch up with these new limbs for some years, and services, schools, telephones and transport, not to mention asphalted roads, may arrive long after the 50,000 or more inhabitants. However, rents here can be as low as £1 ($2.40) a month, and the sparse but adequate homes become their occupier's property after fifty years, assuming that they will still be standing then.

Housing is in fact one of Spain's gravest problems. To the age-old shortage was added the wartime destruction; lack of cash and raw materials left this largely unresolved, and the situation is now aggravated by the flight of peasants to the cities. The 1960 census recorded over 7,600,000 homes, and a shortage of a million. To cope with this, with new population, internal migration and decay of older houses, a National Housing Plan was launched in that year to provide 3,700,000 homes in the next sixteen years. Since then, an average of 195,000 a year have been built. However, the 1967 FOESSA report diagnosed a real 1960 need for 4,335,000 homes at an average of 271,000 a year. For the internal migration figure exceeded all estimates and at the same time real estate boomed in a wave of speculation which did untold damage to the economy, costing the nation perhaps a million dollars a day, more than doubling the cost of housing in central districts, and making sites frequently more expensive than the blocks built on them. In fashionable parts of Madrid site prices per square foot have increased ten times over. Municipal purchase of land fifteen years ago could have prevented all this, but nothing was done. Indeed, city authorities in Spain now speculate with the best. It remains to be seen whether the November 1967 building site tax slapped on to halt speculation in fact does so, or whether it merely gets added to the final price faced by the dweller.

Lack of complete statistics hampers any examination of the housing situation on a nation-wide scale, but reports in the 50s suggested that 40 per cent of the population lacked sewers, while in 1962 20 per cent were without running water. These figures refer essentially to villages. A city problem however is the 600,000 families sharing homes so overcrowded as to constitute a health danger. The rural counterpart is the 400,000 families in caves or shacks utterly unfit for human habitation. Since these estimates are from the early 60s, the emphasis has now probably tilted towards the city crisis.

Global figures for ownership or tenancy are not available, but the FOESSA sample showed 46 per cent of owner-families, with ownership higher in the countryside than in the cities. It is interesting that the drop in new homes for rent in 1965 has lately been reversed, possibly as the result of the 15,000 or so luxury apartments still left vacant and unsold in Madrid. In 1963, 37 per cent of the new flats were for rent and 54 per cent for sale, with 9 per cent for owner-occupiers. By 1965 this had changed to 20, 75 and 5 per cent, but has now started to rectify itself.

The State's contribution to housing is through the Housing Institute of the Ministry of Housing, a body with a budget of £50 million ($120 million) which sponsors some construction directly, but mainly provides private promoters with credits or subsidies according to the classification of the building. In a peak year like 1965, 241,000 of a total of 283,000 homes enjoyed some form of official aid. Of the 247,000 officially-aided homes due for 1968, 150,000 will receive non-repayable subsidies, 72,000 will be authorised to draw credits as Limited Rent class I, and 25,000 as Limited Rent class II (rather more expensive) homes. While the goodwill and endeavour of the State is undeniable, the private promoters turn the legal classifications into something of a fiction, and the State in fact pays out to aid luxury building, a 'limited rent' of £10 ($24) a month being boosted under a dozen different headings to nearer £100 ($240) in some cases. One owner will gather a clutch of State-subsidised homes by putting them under the names of his relatives, and so on.

The tremendous housing shortage encourages the less scrupulous promoters, some of whom draw up contracts which exceed traditional Spanish picaresque practice to enter the terrain of racket. Possibly because of divided spheres of responsibility, the authorities seem unable to do anything about this until the scandal breaks, and even then tend merely to elaborate new rules and regulations instead of simply making the original ones effective. A case in point saw 11,000 families defrauded by a nation-wide building organisation in 1967. Some of the victims had been deprived of their savings for the second time in a few years.

Young couples have to wait for years before marrying with a home over their heads, and the hire purchase may last for three to five years after they manage to scrape up the down payments. A worker earning, say, £500 ($1,200) a year (through overtime and multi-employment), will still have to find £2,500 ($6,000) for a 70 sq-metre flat to take five persons, well away from the city centre. Payment in the commercial field will have to be completed in, say, five years. But for the 30 per cent of Madrid's families estimated by FOESSA to earn less than £400 ($960) a year, commercial solutions are out of the question, and the State housing is insufficient to meet the demand. Nor does Spain have the money to launch an all-out building drive, which would have inflationary effects and tie up capital in non-productive spheres. Moreover, as the construction industry is the first city job for the ex-peasants, more building would draw more workers to the city, who would need more homes. When these were eventually completed, the construction workers would be out of a job.

No easy solution of this problem is in sight, though 1968 marked the Housing Institute's decision to sell many of its directly-owned homes to their occupiers as a means of raising capital for more building. The State supports the 2,177 housing co-operatives which have been formed, and this is indeed a way of cutting out the excess profits otherwise syphoned off by commercial promoters. But the co-ops require energetic and dedicated spirits to launch and run them, something beyond the educational and organisational capacities of the new city immigrants. The 1968 Development Plan (Two) promises doubled expenditure on housing, so a breakthrough on this vital front may be in sight.

HOUSEHOLD EQUIPMENT

The Spain visitors meet seems far better equipped with baths and modern lavatories than many richer European nations. But this is the benefit of starting late and building to please modern and tourist taste. Village Spain is a different proposition, with only a third of rural homes boasting running water; a fifth, bath or shower; less than a tenth with a telephone. These living conditions are another spur to the rural exodus. Reliable recent over-all figures for services are not available, but the FOESSA sample showed 94 per cent of homes with electricity, 62 per cent with running water, 50 per cent with butane gas cylinders, 44 per cent with shower or bath, 32 per cent with heaters, 8 per cent with mains gas, and 4 per cent with central heating. The South, especially, ignores heating equipment. This sample refers to 1965. Since then the butane gas company claims that 80 per cent of Spanish homes now use its squat orange containers.

Spain's domestic revolution is startling in speed because it started from scratch. In 1953 electricity consumption per capita per year was 343 kilowatt hours; by 1966 it was 900 (admittedly puny beside the USA's 5,835), and in 1967 it reached 1,226. Imports would have to be added to Spanish electro-domestic appliance production to obtain per capita ratios, but the home output is in itself indicative. Spain produced 66,000 washing machines in 1959; in 1966, the figure was 361,000. Television sets rose from 25,000 to 526,000 a year over the same period. Refrigerators and radios follow the same pattern, though all save television dropped back severely in 1967 under the effects of recession, and nearly a million bills of exchange (used commonly in Spain for hire purchase) were defaulted in the first half of that year alone. The two-and-a-half thousand homes polled in the FOESSA sample showed 28 per cent with refrigerator, 36 per cent with washing machine, 82 per cent with radio, 32 per cent with TV and 12 per cent with record player. The Spanish Market Yearbook for 1968 shows a 10 per cent rise in nearly all these figures over the three years since the FOESSA sample was made. The figures of the Organisation for Economic Co-opera-tion and Development for 1966 awarded Spain 70 TVs per thousand people in comparison with Britain's 253 and the USA's 372. The same organisation listed Spain as having 95 telephones per thousand to the British 273 and the American 393; a Spanish rise from 12 per cent of families with telephones in 1960 to 23 per cent in 1966. Since then the total (including office telephones) has increased to 3,305,000, or 102 per thousand inhabitants. The backlog to be installed is still half a million, and as telephones in Spain are tied to the subscriber, not the house, a goodly number appear in the telephone book under false names, one more case in which the citizen-tenant has to bend the regulations in self-defence or risk losing his telephone.

By and large, urban workers are better off for consumer durables than middle-class farmers, except in the realm of cars. Bicycles are a case apart, the one item in which wealth does not signify greater abundance, for of course they are essentially a working man's instrument of transportation. In the realm of communications, Spain lags far behind, the fifty-four letters per thousand inhabitants per year being a quarter of the European norm. The newsprint consumption of a mere 7 lb per capita per year is once more only a quarter. However, these two indicators should be placed alongside the large number of telephones to reveal a simple fact. Spaniards prefer to talk.

Domestic servants are still the rule in Spanish middle-class homes, with two and a chauffeur for the upper classes. However, the lure of factory benches is making inroads into the million or so maids and cooks, and their inclusion as part of the master's visible wealth, for tax purposes, may now make the inroads even more drastic.

———

Spain's economy must cope with a geography ranging from the Picos de Europa and a dozen more *sierras*, to the flat rice lands of Valencia.

THE FAMILY BUDGET

The family budget demands mathematical powers in a house-wife, for despite the average family size of 3.75 (plus 0.53 of relatives living in, and 0.8 of living-in servants), it is not uncommon to find broods of ten to fourteen children, especially among the wealthy and devoutly Catholic. The poor, despite the very limited access to birth control methods, have now largely opted for small families. The Spanish housewife has been able to equip her home more fully than ever before, and to improve the nutritive quality of the meals for her family. But she has had to cope with a rise in wholesale prices between 1959 and 1967 of 34 per cent, and in the cost of living over that period of 66 per cent. On the other hand, things cannot have gone too badly for her, if food, which accounted for 55 per cent of the cost of living in 1958, was down to 28 per cent in 1967, so one source has it, while vague ' varied expenses ' rose from around 18 per cent to almost 34 per cent. In the same chart for 1967, clothing etc accounted for 21 per cent (up), housing nearly 9 per cent (up) and expenses, over 7 per cent. However, more plausible altern-

---

Traditional agriculture still outweighs modern industry, but the balance is fast changing.

Tarragona Labour University is meeting this challenge.

E

ative estimates from the Banco de Bilbao give 49 per cent for food in 1958, dropping to 40 per cent in 1967, close to Italy but far behind the USA's 19 per cent and the UK's 27 per cent.

The percentages quoted above tend to fluctuate oddly from year to year, so another angle on budgets is that given by a welfare organisation which calculated that the minimum living income for a couple with two children in Madrid at the end of 1967, was 95,030 pesetas (£570 or $1,360) a year; 44,280 pesetas of which went on food and drink; 3,250 on fuel; 12,370 on housing and domestic expenses; 24,300 on clothing and personal care, and 10,830 on miscellaneous expenses. In many ways Spain is no longer any cheaper than Britain, except where the still inexpensive item known as manhours is decisive in keeping costs down. Materials are more expensive than services, though of course tourists are more interested in services—hotels, restaurants and the like. But shoes have doubled in price over the 60s, and the £10 ($24) ready-made suit is now nearer £18 ($43).

Despite rising prices, Spaniards continue to dress with decorum, the city-dwelling males in suits now verging away from the old short-jacketed Italian style into more daring English long, flared jackets. Girls have always performed miracles to conjure varied wardrobes out of little cash, and they remain a joy to the eye. Of late the trouser-suit has appeared for women, though mini-skirts would be a rasher undertaking in these warm-blooded climates. Beards are flourishing at the universities, and *ye-ye* or pop youth has at last broken through Spanish sartorial conformism with psychedelic shirts. Meanwhile the peasants continue in corduroy and leather windcheaters and black berets screwed to their heads and probably not removed even in bed. Peasant women past a certain age tend to wear black, in mourning not for their lost youth but for lost relatives. Once past a certain age, so many relatives are lost that it is simpler to stay in black the whole time.

FOOD

Spain's daily calorie intake per inhabitant has improved from 2,421 in 1953 to 3,017 in 1967. The national physique has improved likewise. None the less the Spanish diet is still inadequate in the poorer country regions—the bread, olives and sardines of Andalucia—and irrational in the richer regions. For the Spaniard has a tiny breakfast of coffee and a fried batter ring or two at eight or nine o'clock; possibly a session of beer or wine and succulent snacks or *tapas* at two, just before knocking himself out with a four-course lunch followed (in summer, but less widespread than it was) by the *siesta*. And then nothing until a light supper at ten. Wine, naturally, is drunk with meals.

A result of war and post-war rationing is the now universal use of olive oil for cooking, even in the North, as also the heavy fish consumption. The oil, like the garlic, is a Roman relic if we move back to far earlier wars. The Arabs contributed bitter oranges and a wonderful variety of almond-based sweetmeats and confectionery such as Toledo *mazapan*. But while one gets excellent meals in Spain, there is no such thing as Spanish cuisine. The underlying truth about this country is revealed—there is only regional cuisine. Fish dishes in the Basque country, roasts in Castile, rice dishes like the glorious Technicolor *paella* in Valencia, fries in the South, stews and pasties in Galicia, powerful boiled dishes in Asturias and Madrid. Another curiosity about eating in Spain, apart from the lateness of meals, is the fact that vegetables and meat dishes are served consecutively, not combined on one plate, except in cafeterias. Butter is a luxury.

Before giving a national chart of food consumption, one should stress the difference between town and country, with the latter eating twice as much bread and sausage (some of them the splendidly virulent blood-variety) as the former, but only half as much fruit and milk. The Basques and Catalans are great milk-drinkers and meat-eaters, while Andalucians and Extremadurans may hardly touch these items—not only because of their lower standards of living, but because southern or dry Spain is virtually without milch cows (though it seems to have no trouble in breeding fighting bulls and their mates). Ham and chicken play a large rôle in Spanish meat consumption.

Foodstuffs consumption. Lb per capita per year

	1953	1966
Tobacco	2.3	3.8
Wine (gals)	10.3	14.3
Cereals	225.2	222.2
Potatoes	227.4	230.5
Leguminous	15.1	22.4
Fruit and greens	355.9	438.8
Sugar	20.6	43.0
Meat	29.0	61.8
Eggs	10.3	22.4
Fish	39.6	67.3
Milk and derivatives	116.6	140.1
Fats and oils	39.6	50.3

WELFARE

Spain's social security system has taken shape gradually since 1919, adding new forms of coverage to reach the present old age and disability pension; health and maternity services; family allowances; voluntary pension, dowry and schooling schemes and unemployment, industrial illness and work accident benefits.

The many decrees on the subject were unified in 1963, since when the only major innovation has been legislation to bring agricultural workers more or less level with city workers in the extent of coverage available to them.

The State's direct contribution to welfare is small, with just over £28 million ($67.2 million) for Health in the 1968 Budget, while of the £158 million ($379.2 million) for Pensions and Social Security, over £114 million ($273.6 million) was for civil servants' pensions, only £27 million ($64.8 million) for Social

Security, and £16 million ($38.4 million) for charity and general welfare.

Nobody who benefits from the social security system would want to be without it, but, having said as much, it must also be stated that the coverage is neither comprehensive nor automatic, the administration is dispersed, and the amounts offered grossly inadequate. The average annual old age pension paid in 1964 according to some figures (statistical confusion is thick on the entire subject) was but £95 ($228), and the widow's pension £46 ($110). This is not entirely the result of scant means of financing better social services, as independent estimates placed the resources of all the agencies involved at £750 million ($1,800 million). The considerable annual difference in the quotas collected and the sums paid out by the National Social Security Institute (the semi-independent organisation with control from the Ministry of Labour, which is the bedrock of the system), was up till 1966 devoted to capitalisation. In other words, instead of as much going out as came in, with today's workers paying for yesterday's, and tomorrow's for today's, the money accumulated as surplus went on State bonds and National Institute of Industry and private firms' shares, rather like endowments building up income for scholarships. This has now given way to the handout system for the Social Security Institute, though not yet for the Labour Mutuals.

The National Social Security Institute receives the quotas for all types of insurance direct from the 450,000 firms involved (not counting agriculture), which amount to 18.6 per cent of each worker's monthly *basic* wage (an artificial sum which may be only a third of the actual take-home wage). The worker loses only 4.33 per cent, however, from his pay-packet, the remaining 14.27 per cent being met by the employer. (In practice, some small firms find themselves paying out very much more in social security quotas than the apparent 18.6 per cent total indicates.) Workers thus covered number eight million, with over six-and-a-half million family beneficiaries or pensioners. To supplement the allowances available through the National Social Security Institute, many workers join higher-grade employees and the self-employed as members of Mutual Organisations.

The Mutual Organisations are bodies separate from, though parallel to, the National Social Security Institute, and have close ties with the *Sindicatos* or State trade unions. The Self-Employed Mutual Organisation is composed of nineteen sectors of industry and services, while the Labour Mutual Organisations are thirty-three nation-wide and more or less independent bodies which receive monthly quotas of from 8 to 11 per cent of the monthly basic wage, just over half of this being paid by the employer. This percentage is lower than the quota for workers enrolled in the NSSI, but of course, it is a lower percentage of what tend to be the higher wage brackets. These bodies continue with the capitalisation scheme of accumulating resources, and this has led to controversies in which it is said that Spanish labour is in fact the real, though not the effective, owner of most of the country's industrial stocks and shares—by means of enforced savings in the form of social security quotas. Firms contributing to the Mutual Organisations number over 455,000, and the workers (not including the self-employed) close to 5 million. In 1966, the Labour Mutuals were worth about £280 million ($672 million). The National Social Security Institute had resources of £410 million ($984 million). The latter's 1967 income was £500 million ($1,200 million), and its payments notably less, so grumbling from below is audible. However, the resources are being husbanded to meet deficits forecast in the early 70s and the increased cost of Health Insurance, recently extended to agricultural workers. The latter are not yet as fully covered as industrial workers, however.

ALLOWANCES

The actual allowances provided, apart from small lump sums for weddings or deaths, are old age pensions, starting at the age of sixty-five, if the individual has already paid five years of quotas. If the individual is not a Mutual member, he or she receives £3 ($7.20) a month; if a Mutual pension is due, however, the Social Security Institute provides only £1 10s ($3.60) a month. Widows of pensioners or of those qualified for pensions receive half the above sums if themselves over sixty-five. In all cases pensioners and their widows must not earn income apart from these pensions (a sardonic clause). With the various Mutual Organisations' pensions, however, the amounts rise considerably, and vary from 40 to 90 per cent of the wage average fixed by each Labour Mutual, the lower percentage if the member wishes to retire at the age of 60, the higher at the age of 70. As well as Spaniards, these organisations automatically cater for regularly employed Hispano-Americans, Portuguese, Andorrans, Filipinos, and Brazilians, and any nationals whose governments have social security agreements with Spain.

Family allowances come into operation for all offspring or dependants under the age of fourteen, and range from about 7s (84 cts) a month for one child, to £7 10s ($17) a month for ten, increasing at an astronomical rate thereafter to encourage vast families. But while the mother of twelve gets £27 ($64), plus another £18 ($43) for each subsequent child, a widow on her own receives 5s (60 cts) a month, and £3 ($7.20) a month if she has eight children to bring up. The same rates apply to orphans.

Schooling allowances of £18 ($43) a year or more are also provided for orphans automatically, while higher education students of all categories can take out an insurance with quotas paid partly by the Ministry of Education and Science, to cover a wide range of family and other disasters that could otherwise interrupt studies.

Disability is basically part of the Old Age scheme, and unemployment will be dealt with in Chapter 5. Variations on the main social security set-up are found in the agricultural sphere where regularly-employed workers contribute a monthly 6s (72 cts), (seasonal workers less, and the self-employed a minimal amount) and landowners are taxed independently on the annual turnover of their property, and contribute 10s 6d ($1.26) per worker per month. Domestic servants have their own mutual society, and contribute 5s (60 cts) a month. Civil servants and the military have their own separate systems.

Only a few of the very biggest firms run pension schemes for their employees, so one would imagine that many fathers of a family would turn to life insurance policies to cater for their old age or demise. However, such is the generalised belief in the rapid depreciation of money that the 97 life insurance companies have only 870,000 policy holders. Another aspect of the social security system, as run at present, is that in order to avoid maximum commitments in paying out their share of the quotas, many firms find it cheaper to employ too few workers and make them do overtime than to engage larger staff for each of whom new quotas would have to be paid. In other cases, and not only in the building trade, workers are hired on six-month contracts only to avoid their classification as ' fixed ' with all its implications. In some Andalucian olive factories, women have been working for twenty years on successive six-month contracts.

For all the shortcomings noted, however, it must be granted that a modern and fairly extensive social security system is a creation owed mainly to post-war Spain. But it was set up at a moment of national poverty, and neither administration nor the allowances provided have matched the frenetic leap in the economy and especially in the cost of living. An increase in the sums offered may be seen in 1969.

THE NATIONAL HEALTH SERVICE

The aspect of social security likely to show an increasing deficit is the obligatory Health Insurance scheme, which covers all workers earning less than £344 a year in basic (not real) wages, plus their dependants. This income limit is due to be raised and may even be abolished. Running it all is the National Social Security Institute, but working through the Mutual societies, the *Sindicatos*, and numerous private collaborating agencies. The benefits for the sick are 75 per cent of their basic wage, plus 75 per cent of family allowance for 39 weeks in a year. Medical services and medicaments in hospitals are free, but hospitalisation lasts only twelve weeks. Longer periods of coverage are available only to those with membership of the Mutual societies. Maternity benefits accrue after nine months of coverage (six of which must have been in the previous twelve months), and include medical care from the sixth month of pregnancy, hospitalisation, 75 per cent of earnings during a rest period of six weeks (voluntary) before birth, and six weeks (compulsory) after birth. Workers' wives covered by family allowances also receive maternity benefits.

The SOE, as the health scheme is called, has around seventy hospitals of its own, some of them mammoth creations like the Madrid La Paz complex and its Barcelona counterpart, but many other hospitals are used for SOE patients. Contributors and their dependants are affiliated to their nearest outpatients clinic (nearly 800 according to one source) and to a doctor to whose list they are added without option, and for whom their name means is 6d (18 cts) per family card. In populous city districts, each general practitioner at a complex for outpatients may have 650 cards on his list. As he may only have an hour to spend on them before rushing off to his next job in private or company medicine, this tends to produce five-minute in-out consultations unless the patient can clearly demonstrate symptoms requiring the attention of a specialist.

Virtually two-thirds of Spain's 40,000 or so doctors have some connection with the SOE, and the scheme also draws heavily on the 3,000 dentists, 5,000 midwives and a number of the 21,000 *practicantes*, a species of sub-doctor mainly concerned with applying treatment and needles. In addition, the country, but not the SOE, has about 7,000 vets and 13,000 pharmacists. The latter are currently incensed by the SOE attempt to save money by bulk-buying medicaments from the manufacturers and providing them directly at clinics to patients who pay only 10 per cent of the cost. The potential business loss to the dispensaries is considerable, as the national pill, injection and suppository mania (Spaniards are never happy unless over-dosed with antibiotics; Dr Fleming has streets and statues everywhere) produced a 1967 medicaments bill of over £100 million ($240 million).

The drawbacks of the SOE are the usual Spanish ones of

rigid administration and under-paid and dissatisfied staff. The doctors fume at their low wages (£24 ($57) monthly is normal at lower grades) and are forced to skimp the job. Meanwhile, the papers constantly carry tales of black farce as desperate relatives in a taxi take a dying man from one hospital to another, all of which pass the buck and the future corpse because he is a member of a different mutual society or the like. The ultramodern La Paz showpiece has a heliport for duties formerly entrusted to storks, but so few night emergency operation doctors that appendixes and the like are frozen and told to come back some other time. And as I was writing this book a construction worker from the site next door came swinging perilously across the girders seven storeys up to beg me to fill in forms for his sick son on my typewriter. They were beautifully and clearly hand-written (probably by the child's teacher, as the man was illiterate), but unless typed no benefits were available for the child.

HOSPITALS

The available hospital statistics are out of date as well as confused, but the 1963 ratio of 4.4 beds per thousand inhabitants represented a doubling of the ratio of ten years before. Even so, it fell behind the Greek and Portuguese levels, though these two countries normally lag behind Spain in all economic indicators. Of the 1,640 hospitals of 1963 (things have improved considerably since then), nearly three hundred were general, and of the rest, half were surgical, over 200 were maternity homes, 26 childrens', 124 mental, and 60 anti-tuberculosis sanatoria. The biggest hospitals are those belonging to the provincial authorities and the SOE, while municipalities also run numerous and fairly large welfare hospitals, as well as the city *Casas de Socorro* or emergency first-aid and care stations. The Red Cross, the Church and the National Movement also play a considerable rôle in running their own hospitals, while the numerous private clinics cater for the more wealthy patients, who pay for everything out

of their own pockets unless they subscribe £1 ($2.40) a month or
so to the many private health insurance organisations which provide top doctors and all save medicaments and hospitalisation
charges free when the time comes. Most of the private clinics
provide private rooms with two beds, so that a member of the
family may stay with the patient. As Spaniards fear solitude and
silence almost more than death itself, this human touch is psycho-
logically and therapeutically shrewd.

DOCTORS

The doctor per inhabitants ratio has improved in recent years
to reach 826 in 1967, not far off the European norm. However,
the big cities are exactly twice as well off for doctors as the rural
zones, even when we allow for the fact that perhaps 20 per cent
of the doctors in Madrid and Barcelona do not actually practise.
In the olden days, Spanish universities seemed to produce only
lawyers and doctors, but today the doctor-figures mislead, as a
large proportion of graduates in medicine are South Americans
fleeing the political chaos of their native universities in search of a
degree. After, say, seven years of learning medicine out of two or
three prescribed books, chanted at him in a class of 600 if he can
get a place and if the professor bothers to turn up, the Spanish
doctor tends to make his first contact with human bodies and
beings after graduation rather than before. This may explain
the eager curiosity with which the knife is wielded in Spain,
though commercial reasons enter into it as well. For, once out
of humble parishes into fashionable practice, Spanish doctors'
fees are not modest, and the top surgeons can charge astro-
nomical sums for the more complicated exercises on wealthy
bodies. Not only can, but do, even if in a kind of Robin Hood
compensation, these aces with the scalpel will then operate
entirely free on the poor. Professional etiquette is watched over
by the provincial and central colleges of doctors, while health
as a whole (apart from the SOE) is the responsibility of the
Health Department at the Ministry of the Interior.

Inhabitants per dentist and doctor in various countries
1960

Country	Dentists	Doctors
Sweden	1,470	1,008
United States	1,920	765
England	3,700	1,104
France	3,000	910
Spain	10,869	829

Note: in 1967, Spain had one dentist per 11,289 inhabitants, and one doctor per 826.

Sources: National Institute of Economic and Social Research, *Health and Welfare Services in Britain in* 1965 (C.U.P. 1966 p 45).

UN Statistical Yearbook (New York 1963 p 603).

Beneficiaries of Health Scheme in Spain (SOE)

Years	% of SOE affiliates of total population	Number of beneficiaries per 1,000 inhabitants
1960	45	437
1964	52	511
1967	54	540

Source: Instituto Nacional de Estadistica

THE HEALTH OF THE NATION

The Health Department has been responsible for highly successful anti-polio and other vaccination drives. The illnesses causing the 867,000 hospitalisations recorded in the *Anuario Estadistico* for 1964 (not necessarily the real total), showed tuberculosis accounting for 21,000, malign tumours for 12,000, eye problems for 18,000, apart from such old faithfuls as appendicitis and tonsilitis, pregnancy and its complications. Deaths in 1963 showed heart ailments leading with 41,700, followed by cancer with nearly 40,000, and tuberculosis with 6,700. In recent years malaria, yellow fever and typhus deaths have been eliminated.

Leprosy persists to a minor degree, though mainly in the depressed South and Canary Islands. Trachoma is on its way to extinction, possibly because Spain, two of whose sons have been Nobel medicine prize-winners this century, has an extraordinarily advanced tradition of eye specialisation, notably the Barraquer clinic in Barcelona.

Of Spanish health in general, one may say that apart from a million and a half rheumatics and nine hundred thousand civil disabled, and 19,279 blind grouped in a remarkably enterprising organisation called ONCE, together with growing incidence of executives' diseases (nervous and coronary, brought on by stress, rage, frustration and alarm), the Spaniard's main preoccupation is his digestion and his liver, if to a lesser degree than his French neighbours. Men lose hair young, but teeth are excellent, perhaps because few people eat sweets. In any case, an additional incentive to survival is the rising cost of death, which in Madrid ranges from the humblest £4 ($9.6) funeral to a Technicolor spectacular for £350 ($890).

The non-health aspect of welfare is catered for by 1,400 establishments ranging from old people's homes to orphanages and centres for the rehabilitation of sub-normal children. Local and provincial authorities share this task with specialised organisations to care for children, to protect girls and the like. The National Movement has its Social Aid branch, and the Church, quite apart from the many homes run by religious orders, has the effective Caritas operation on a nation-wide basis. In some cases Dickensian conditions prevail, but this contrasts with ultramodern homes such as the old people's centre outside Madrid with modern flatlets for old couples, or the San Juan de Dios township for the subnormal being built for Seville. The State devotes about £3.6 million ($8.6 million) to the needy young and old, catering in some degree for 150,000, or about half the number applying for aid and care. We have no knowledge of the further numbers who need care but despair of applying.

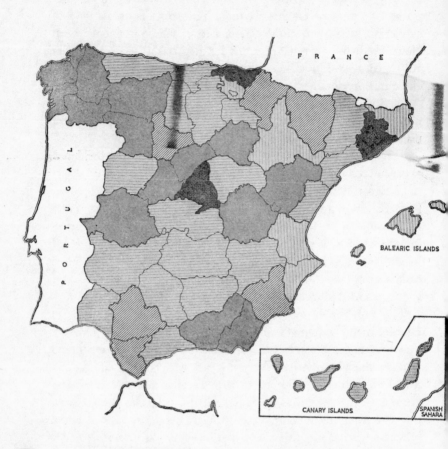

Post-industrial provinces: 14% or less of labour force in agriculture
Industrial: 15%–24%
Semi-industrial: 25%–34%
Under-developed: 35%–49%
Pre-industrial: 50% or more of labour force in agriculture

5

How They Work

THE Spanish economy is a violently controversial subject, with various interested parties reacting to it with triumph, wild praise, intense pessimism, prophecies of woe, criticism of the built-in structural defects, calls for nationalisation, calls for removing State controls, calls for planning, accusations that planning has failed miserably. The group of enlightened 'technocrat' ministers at the ministries dealing with economics (Planning Bureau, Finance, Commerce, Industry; and Agriculture at some distance from the first four) advocate integration into the Common Market as a necessary blast of competition which would end the inefficient home-market orientation of too much industry. It would also, they tacitly believe, blow Spain into modern Europe politically as well as economically.

The men of this persuasion, moderate neo-capitalists, triggered the consumer boom of the sixties, and ended the previous period of autarchy and excessive State control of imports, wages and trade which had brought Spain in the 50s to virtual bankruptcy through inflation. The boom, based essentially on tourism income and emigrants' remittances, itself ran into inflation, and the First Development Plan, its chosen instrument, ended its four-year cycle with the unexpected devaluation of November 1967. This was to some measure a moment of revenge for the Falangists of the discredited autarchy period, and also the many industrialists petrified by the thought of European dumping under an association with the Common Market.

Leaving aside the exaggerated polemics, however, we can

safely say that Spain's recent economic progress has been spectacular, the growth rate beaten only by Japan. On the other
hand, the solidity of this development, largely a by-product of
European prosperity (tourism and emigrant workers in foreign
factories) is questionable.

Not until 1950 was the Spanish economy back to its pre-
Civil War level. The conflict killed half a million men, and the
Bank of Spain's 510 tons of gold were shipped to Russia by the
Republic, where at the time of writing they still rest. The destruction of war was followed by the privations of World War
and the economic boycott which followed. The first stage of re-
construction in isolation was from 1940 to 1953, with an annual
accumulative increase in the national income of 3.7 per cent.
With American aid, expansion started in 1954, alongside inflation, and ground to a halt with the Stabilisation Plan of 1959.
With devaluation then and austerity, but also liberalisation of
trade, and the European Common Market boom across the
frontier, the 1954-9 expansion rate of 4.6 per cent was out-
stripped easily, and 7.5 per cent has been the rate yearly until the
1967 pause.

———

The really fertile soil in Spain is the Mediterranean sand with
its annual crop of foreign tourists.

THE NATIONAL INCOME

The national income in 1967 amounted to 1,389,352 million pesetas (over £8,300 million, $19,920 million) in current pesetas, contrasting with the 501,974 million (£3,000 million or $7,200 million) of 1958. In constant value pesetas of 1958, the new income figure would be 826,062 million pesetas (£4,956 or $11,894 million). Over the same period, the per capita income rose from 16,846 pesetas ($281 or £100 at pre-1967 devaluation rates) to 42,841 pesetas at current values. This would have carried Spain past the $700 mark, but the 1967 devaluation sent it down the scale again to $612 (£252).

A feature marking Spain off from the fully developed countries is a wages and salaries share of between 55 and 60 per cent, as opposed to the 75 per cent or so of industrialised nations. Another significant feature is the imbalance in the regional share of the economy. It was in 1962 that statistics at last revealed that while Madrid and Barcelona provinces each earned around 15 per cent of the national total, there were fifteen provinces with less than 1 per cent, and twenty-five with between 1 and 2 per cent.

School for many, exercise and excursions for only a few. Sport is not yet a practical and psychological part of Spanish education.

F

Since then, the rich provinces have grown richer and the poor richer too, but not strikingly so. Per capita income in Madrid, Barcelona and the Basque country is still three times greater than in the poorest parts of Galicia and Andalucia. With Madrid as an isolated patch of development thanks to its status as the capital, the weight of Spain's economy is seen to reside on the line drawn by the river Ebro from the Basque country in the north to Catalonia in the north-east, one region facing Britain across the waters of Biscay, the other profiting from Mediterranean traffic, and both from the nearness of France and technological and business consciousness.

IMPORTS AND EXPORTS

Spain has one of the world's finest trade deficits, $2,120 million in 1967, though this was $217 million less than in 1966. Despite this alarming gap the nation's gold and currency reserves were still, in mid-1968, healthy at $1,090 million, of which $785 million were in gold. These reserves tell the real story of Spanish development, for throughout the 40s and 50s the reserves had oscillated around $120 to $200 million, before dropping hideously to $65 million in 1958, the danger signal which led to stabilisation. Thereafter they shot upwards to reach $1,508 million in 1965, descending slowly but gracefully from that high point.

When a country imports $3,530 millions' worth as Spain did in 1967 (nearly $1,000 million in capital equipment, over $500 million in foodstuffs), and exports only $1,411 million ($632 million in foodstuffs), then some kind fairy has to close the gap, if the balance of payments deficit is to be a mere $156 million, as it turned out. Incidentally, 36 per cent of Spain's imports are from the Common Market, 16 per cent from EFTA (a third of them from Britain), and 18 per cent from the USA and Canada. By contrast, Spain's exports are 32 per cent to the Common Market, 20 per cent to EFTA and 16 per cent to the USA and Canada (all 1967 figures). The East European bloc accounts for just under 2 per cent of imports, and over 5 per cent of exports (as imports nearly triple exports, this means that Spanish-East Europe trade is virtually balanced in value). Despite all the rhetoric, trade with Ibero-America is a mere 10 per cent of Spanish imports and 14 per cent of exports. Africa and Asia feature even less significantly.

We have mentioned the kindly agents who close Spain's balance of payments gap. In 1967 they took the form of 17,858,000 tourists, of whom 14,810,000 were foreigners carrying passports (ie long-stay, heavier-spending visitors); only 2.5 per cent up on 1966, admittedly, but the pattern of Spanish tourism seems to show leaps followed by pauses. Thus, from under eleven million in 1963 to fourteen in 1964, little rise in 1965, then a leap to the seventeen million-plus in 1967. By all standards, the rise from one and a quarter million in 1951 to the eighteen to nineteen million expected in 1968 (stimulated by Spanish devaluation), is dramatic. Income from tourism in 1967 was calculated roughly at just above the $1,250 million received in 1966. By mid-1968 the hotel beds available were around 400,000, and camping sites proliferated. The Balearic Islands, Canaries, Costa Brava and Costa del Sol were the main attractions, but, intelligently stimulated by the Ministry of Information and Tourism (and prices and abuses sternly controlled and checked by it), several new coasts have come into fashion, as have promising winter sports resorts.

In 1967, seven-and-a-half million of the tourists to Spain were French, nearly two million were British, while Germans and Portuguese accounted for about one-and-a-quarter million apiece. Americans were only three-quarters of a million, but their spending habits make them more welcome than twice their number of self-contained French campers and caravanners.

There are fears that the 1967 American austerity measures may cut down the number of tourists from the States, and also the level of American investment, a second and most important aid for the Spanish economy. Of the $411 million invested in 1967, 44 per cent came from the United States, followed by Switzerland with 24 per cent (not necessarily Swiss money, of course). Britain invested only 3.3 per cent. This is not all one-way traffic, though, as the foreign firms can export their profits and their capital again in currency whenever they wish.

Finally, the remittances and money brought or sent back by Spanish workers abroad came to $414 million by November 1967, slightly down on the previous year. This drop reminded Spaniards that two-thirds of their foreign income was in the nature of invisible exports, which were in turn the reflection of foreign prosperity and subject to its fluctuations. In this, of course, Spain is not unique, and should not take the puritanical view that exporting services instead of merchandise is morally blameworthy. For industry suffers as much from international slump as services.

FINANCE

Finance within Spain comes only to a very reduced degree from the stock exchanges active in Madrid, Bilbao and Barcelona, perhaps 5 per cent of the value of the companies quoted. This is because investors fear the effect of inflation, while the companies get their money from the banks, which not only give credit but in most cases own large packets of shares in the firms themselves. Forbidden to give overdrafts to private individuals, Spain's private banking system acts as merchant or industrial bank as well as commercial, and so virtually controls the economy, and, some of its opponents claim, the nation as well. Private banking provides around two-thirds of finance, against about 22 per cent from Savings Banks and 14 per cent from State credit agencies. Brooding over the entire system is the Bank of Spain, nationalised in 1962. The Savings Banks are a growing force in the land, and represent the savings of the workers. Thirteen of the Savings Banks in the Confederation handle 60 per cent of their business, and by the end of 1966, deposits in their Confederation came to £1,625 million ($3,900 million) or 42 per cent as much as the amount then held by the private banks.

In 1967, Spain had 119 banks, 13 of them nation-wide in

scope, while the remainder were regional, local or specialised. The 13 big ones handle 80 per cent of the credit, and among these, the Big Five dominate the picture completely (Banco Español de Credito, deposits £708 million ($1,699 million), Banco Hispano-Americano, Banco Central, Banco de Bilbao and Banco de Vizcaya, the last named about half the size of the first). On the other hand, all Spanish private banking only amounts to a fraction of the Bank of America alone.

Commonly seen as economic villains by some Spanish experts and some Spanish demagogues, the banks refrain from under-cutting one another, and offer little that can be interpreted as service to the client, whether an individual or a firm—unless the latter is partly owned and mainly controlled by the bank in question. Credit is extended at high interest only to enterprises whose profitability is one thousand per cent certain. The excess profits are disguised in the building of luxurious new branch offices. Deposits held by the banks have increased eight times over in the last fifteen years, and the banks' own shares have increased in value in much the same proportion.

In the early 60s, a merger plan between numbers two and three of the Big Five was vetoed by the Government, but the Finance Ministry's rather hurried attempt in the summer of 1968 to weaken bank control of industry through interlocking directorships, had its teeth drawn (predictably) by the Cortes.

INDUSTRY

Spanish industry almost seems to be a post-1940 phenomenon. It did exist in the 19th century, of course, but as a sickly child, sustained by rigid protectionism against foreign products, while financed to a very great extent by foreign capital. Spain's back-wardness in this sphere was a combination of mental attitudes and lack of ready power sources, allied to high illiteracy (over half the male population, almost three-quarters of the female in 1887), a weak home market and indifference to science and technology. The bourgeois revolution had come too late. In addition, coal from Britain was better and cheaper than from Asturias.

The turn of the century saw the rise of Spanish banking, thanks largely to funds repatriated from the lost colonies of Cuba, Puerto Rico and the Philippines, and marked the beginning of a bank-ownership of industry which is now extreme. The Primo de Rivera period (of 1923-30) saw industrial advance, but the slump and then the Civil War halted progress. Because of the World War that followed, and Spain's subsequent isolation, the aim was autarchy—self-sufficiency—to some extent a necessity for survival in a hostile environment, but also liable to produce anti-economic industry.

The method chosen to stimulate Spain's industrial development was the National Institute of Industry, a giant State holding company which fathered factories and enterprises in several key sectors, thus laying down a significant groundwork even in the years of scarce raw materials, when Spain had no foreign currency to indulge in imports; a situation which changed for the better with official American aid in 1953 (and privately, a year or so earlier).

Financed originally by the State, and now through bonds placed with the Savings Banks and other sources of cash, the INI, as it is always known, is worth about £540 ($1,296) million, employing 170,000 workers and staff in the 70 undertakings of which it owns 17 outright, has a majority share in 32, and a minority share in the rest. The INI firms have 20 per cent of electricity, 36 per cent of coal, 25 per cent of steel, and around half of such other basic sectors as aluminium, fertilisers, petrol, shipbuilding and motor manufactures. There is an increasing tendency for its firms to pass under private enterprise domination, and the placing of the Institute under the Ministry of Industry in 1968 was thought to be another move in this direction and away from the nationalised competition with private enterprise desired by some sections of the nation and press. Designed to set up basic industry where private enterprise feared to tread, the INI has been attacked by industrialists as a fearsome rival, and by Falangists as an accomplice of Spain's traditional capitalism in that it delicately refrained from ruthless competition. Many good points cannot be denied it, notably the Aviles steelworks, but the great question, as so often in Spain, is whether it has saved the country more than it has cost the country, for lack of business sense is commonly attributed to it from several sides of the controversy.

For the rest, Spanish industry suffers from extremes—thousands of factories and workshops too small and technically backward to produce good quality material cheaply enough, and a few mammoths which tend to set up monopolies and hold the country to ransom behind protectionist tariffs, making high profit from outdated equipment and inefficient organisation without a thought for the morrow. In the 60s equipment at least improved, but doubts persist about the organisation and spirit of enterprise. It is widely believed that the accounts of Spain's largest firms contain many skeletons, and that for years now the attitude has been one of gather ye dividends while ye may. One result of this is the absence of Spanish research and technology, in default of which manufacturers simply buy a foreign patent (frequently not the most up to date and with an export ban built into the deal), produce it expensively, and pay out royalties for ever more.

On the other hand, industrialists plead that they can never make long-term plans of a constructive nature because of the uncertainty generated by the red-tape surrounding their every move and the constant flow of decrees and ministerial orders changing the rules of the game every five minutes. At all events, the result is that with one of Europe's top half-dozen motor industries, there is no Spanish-designed car.

FUEL AND POWER

Power has been one of the Spanish success stories since the 50s, when electricity cuts ceased to be the norm. Coal, however, is on the decline because of generally poor quality and difficult extraction, and the fifteen-and-a-third million tons of 1967 is in fact lower than the figure for the late 50s. As rail and other consumers abandon coal, the Asturian mines have to think increasingly of supplying thermic power stations. The more than 500 mining firms would in many cases welcome nationalisation. A half-way step has been the creation of a large mixed consortium called Hunosa, with finance to rationalise and re-equip the more viable mines.

Despite modest oil-strikes in the north and off-shore prospection in the south, Spain is a non-oil-producing nation with annual imports of about 20.6 million tons, refined by seven refineries in which Spanish groups are associated with the big foreign oil combines. Distribution is in the hands of a para-Statal monopoly called Campsa. Spain has started barter oil deals with Russia, and is developing interests in the oilfields of Libya and Kuwait.

Electricity output has risen dramatically from the 2,681 million kilowatt-hours of 1931 to 40,000 million kilowatt-hours in 1967, with thermic stations accounting for almost 18,000 million kilowatt-hours. Both INI and the big private electricity firms (largely bank-owned) form part of the Unesa and Ofile organisations for regulating electricity supply. Various companies have joined up to launch nuclear-powered stations of ever greater installed capacity near Madrid, Burgos, Tarragona and Bilbao.

MINERALS

In the sphere of mining, economist Ramon Tamames thinks that the widespread belief in Spain's mineral riches is no longer true, and that only times of international shortage and crisis bring much of Spain's capacity into demand. Iron ore may escape this judgment with estimated reserves of 1,300 million tons. Lead is present in quantity, but mined at high cost to produce about 53,000 tons a year. Spanish zinc near Santander is of high quality, as is the copper obtained from the pyrites of Rio Tinto near Huelva, while tin, aluminium and the significant wolfram, manganese and mercury add to Spain's list of metals.

The Almaden mercury mines are famous, producing between 1,500 and 2,000 tons a year, 90 per cent of the output going to the United States.

Spain also produces salt and potassium sulphate, and if the peninsular phosphate deposits are unimportant, the Spanish Sahara has reserves estimated at 1,715 million tons. Pyrites, largely around Rio Tinto, are an important export. Spain is thought to possess over half the world's deposits.

IMPORTANT INDUSTRIES

Spain was late in developing a steel industry, and when it came the Basque country was the area chosen, not Asturias (which had coal) because of swift and cheap supply from Britain. The oldest-established steelworks of any size is the Bilbao Altos Hornos de Vizcaya, whose predominance was challenged by the INI's Ensidesa works at Aviles on the Asturian coast. Other Asturian works have come together with Krupp capital to form Uninsa. American capital is heavily involved with Altos Hornos. The consumer boom of the 60s exceeded the production capacity of Spain's foundries, and led to heavy importation of pig iron and steel. However, there are signs that re-equipment and management changes are stirring the Spanish steel industry, and output has doubled throughout the decade to reach the 1967 total of 4.25 million tons of steel, apart from iron and rolled products.

Cement has also received a boost in recent years, rising at around 10 per cent a year to reach 13.3 million tons in 1967, almost all of it Portland type. Chemicals are improving likewise, though with the excessive number of some 7,000 firms.

Electro-domestics and other consumer durables such as vehicles have doubled since 1960; in the case of television sets and refrigerators the increase has been from five to ten times, with TVs now over the half-million mark for yearly output. The other items have fallen back somewhat from the 1966 figures, and even cars, expected to beat 350,000 in 1967, reached only about

275,000; lorries and vans 90,000. In 1950, of course, Spain's car output was nil. That year saw the foundation of SEAT, which manufactures Fiat cars under licence, and still has over half the Spanish market, despite later comers such as Renault, Citroen, Chrysler (owning 77 per cent of Barreiros) and the Morris range produced at Pamplona. Lorries have tie-ups with Austin, Leyland and German makes, while Land-Rovers are also manufactured in Spain. The Leyland-influenced Pegaso lorries sell well abroad. Spain has some excellent light motor-cycles, but production of these is falling as the consumer spurns two wheels in favour of four.

Shipbuilding is an unexpectedly strong Spanish sector, with over 400,000 gross registered tons launched in 1967, a quarter of this for export. Spain is one of the world's top oil tanker builders, and the first Spanish 150,000-tonner will soon be tackled. Mergers are the order of the day in the major yards, and the State helps with concerted action schemes to renew equipment. Meanwhile, civil construction employs nearly a million workers in nearly 30,000 firms, some of them giants, most of them one-horse affairs with hopelessly low mechanisation levels. Housing is sensitive to the fluctuations of the economy.

Textiles are an important Spanish manufacture, by far the greater part of them centred on and around Barcelona, though the wool side is more diversified throughout the country, as befits one of Spain's great medieval industries. (The merino sheep is a Spaniard.) While the Catalan towns of Sabadell and Tarrasa carry the weight of textiles, cloth from Bejar near Salamanca is of the very finest. Since the war Spain's wool garment consumption has dropped, and is now a third of the OECD countries' average. Leather and footwear is an expanding export trade, with tourists buying suede jackets and imaginatively-designed shoes. The footwear trade is clustered on Majorca and the Levante coast, and could make greater strides were the myriad firms merged into competitive combines. This is something which holds good for numerous sectors of Spanish industry and commercialisation—a nostalgic or unadvantageous hanging-on to artisan-sized workshops and enterprises in the teeth of rationality and competitiveness. But then it could be that many Spaniards, at least in the older generations, feel no great enthusiasm for rationality and competition. They ride their firms individually, and for profit, but the public is not served.

AGRICULTURE

' Spain,' it was said recently, ' has ceased to be an agricultural country.' Rather we could say that Spain's agriculture is no longer adequate. The industrial and services boom of the sixties has thrown cruel stress on the failings of a traditional agriculture, for it has drawn the peasant population to Spanish or other European cities. This has at once emptied the villages of manpower, leaving only the very old, the very young, and the womenfolk. However, the influx of new inhabitants into the cities, and the tourists along the coasts, have created a vast demand for foodstuffs of a variety, quality and quantity that the countryside is incapable of providing. What it can provide is doubled in price by the crazy chain of commercialisation intermediaries seeking high profit and often letting the supply go bad for lack of refrigerated storage. The deficit, especially in meat, has been met by costly imports. So agricultural Spain has become a food importer.

But at the same time Spain is a major food exporter. Valencia is famed for oranges, Andalucia for olives and olive oil, Jerez, La Mancha and the Rioja are great wine-producing areas. Murcia and the La Rioja-Navarre area have brisk fruit and vegetable canning industries. Despite lack of rain in many areas and poor soil in others, Spain's agricultural problems can be solved, though they have proved resistant till now.

Agriculture's share of the national income is generally around 15 per cent and the charts for the 1967 season show cattle accounting for just over 22 per cent of the agricultural total, followed by cereals at 12 per cent, fruit also 12 per cent, greens at 10 per cent, and everything else—eggs, milk, potatoes, wine and oil all ranging around 6 per cent each, which with a number of lesser items amounted to a value of about £1,325 ($3,280) million. What is remarkable is that wheat, cereals and legumens, producing just over 12 per cent of the agrarian product, take up 60 per cent of the cultivated land. State over-commitment to wheat, relic of hard times and rationing, which guarantees high prices for surpluses, contributes to this situation at a time when bread consumption is dropping and when fodder cereals are far more necessary to help the livestock drive.

Fruit is a profitable concern, and Spain's varied climate produces even tropical varieties, while the Canary Islands abound with bananas and tomatoes, traditional exports to Britain, like Valencia's oranges and other citrus fruits. Today, however, the Common Market and Eastern Europe are the main buyers of Spanish oranges and mandarins, lemons and grapefruit. Crops of 1,200,000 tons are normal, but Spain has fallen behind competitor countries in the Mediterranean in grading, selecting varieties, and rationalising commercialisation abroad. An average to good year may earn Spain £60 ($144) million from citrus fruits, 70 per cent of this from the Common Market. It is ironic that British housewives get better Spanish oranges than Spanish housewives, and at half the price. The same prices apply with bananas, and almost the same with grapes, another big export, largely from Almeria in Andalucia, a town which thinks of London and Liverpool rather than Madrid.

Wine is one of Spain's great undertakings as well as one of her great joys for the visitor. Nowhere else in the world is the ordinary table wine from the barrel so strong, so good and so cheap—at around five cents the pint. Sherries and the milder, softer Montillas are between 5s (60 cts) and 6s 6d (78 cts) the bottle; the brandies between 6s (72 cts) and 10s (120 cts) the bottle, and though not really the same thing as French brandy, some of the less extensively advertised ones are still excellent. Spanish champagne has to be called 'sparkling wine' in Britain as the result of a French lawsuit, but tastes none the worse for the label. Just over four million acres are under grapes in Spain, with La Mancha the largest area, though its light-coloured Valdepeñas is not known abroad. The Valencian and Catalan coasts also produce a lot of wine, especially Tarragona; the Prioratos are the most famous, reaching eighteen degrees. Jerez and its surroundings contain the celebrated *bodegas* of a dozen or more sherry firms, often with English and Irish names, reflecting a trade which tickled the palate of Sir John Falstaff long ago and now exports more sherry to Britain than to the rest of the world put together, though sales to the United States are increasing strongly. Galicia produces tart purple *ribeiro* wine, the Basque country the delicate *chacolí*, while La Rioja offers the finest table wines in Spain, rich Burgundy types with a full bouquet.

If Spain is one of the world's great wine countries, the olive crop is second to none, and the Mediterranean strip under olives has nearly doubled in three-quarters of a century to reach five-and-a-half million acres, especially around Jaen in Andalucia. Always used as the cooking oil in the South, it replaced animal fats in the cuisine of Spain's North during the rationing and isolation period after the war. Spain's annual crop, varying from 400,000 to 600,000 metric tons, is usually about 40 per cent of the world total, and its export brings in about £42 ($102) million.

Spain also produces sugar beet, tobacco and cotton in the southern regions, all of which help with the balance of payments. Where imports of food upset this panorama however, is in the realm of livestock. Absence of grass in the southern half of the country for much of the year, lack of fodder cereal-growing and the spread of forestry, affect meat supply, while higher city living standards and millions of foreign tourists with large appetites affect meat demand. Spain's livestock is diminishing with regard to traction animals as farming becomes more mechanised; however, the meat production is rising steadily, and the Development Plan has stressed concerted action schemes whereby the State helps stockbreeders to improve the strain of their cattle. In 1967 pork and ham amounted to 450,000 tons, chicken more than 266,000, beef and veal 215,000 and mutton 122,000 tons. Milk output is in the region of 628 million gallons, eggs 550 million dozen, and wool 30,000 metric tons.

FORESTRY

Of Spain's 126 million or so acres, over half are tree-clad, even though timber and cork's contribution to the national income is slight by comparison. However, this situation is more properly one of erratically or inadequately tree-clad areas, the result of centuries of random felling for shipbuilding or firewood. To remedy soil erosion and to improve rainfall, a big refforestation drive was launched in Spain after the Civil War, and this will in the long run improve Spain's timber per forest acre yield, now only a quarter of the European average. Reafforestation since 1940 has covered three million acres.

FISHERIES

Fishery is big business in Spain, and the country was the number eight fishery power in the world as long ago as 1964, almost certainly moving up the scale since then. The offshore Mediterranean fishing fleet is composed basically of small craft which supply fishing villages with their sustenance, without greatly affecting the national economy. But the fishing fleet of over half a million tons (gross registered) is establishing itself deep in the Atlantic with refrigerated storage ships, while not neglecting the rich areas of Galicia and Biscay. Fish, molluscs and crustaceans have multiplied six times over in the last forty years to produce the current Spanish annual catch of one-and-a-half million tons, a fifth of which goes straight to the canning factories. The main species caught are hake and sole, cod and tunny, not forgetting the abundant sea-food of the north-west.

THE AGRARIAN PROBLEM

In Spain agriculture is not purely an economic matter, however, but an acute social and political one stemming from the nature of land tenure. The key word here is the *latifundio* or large estate of over 617 acres, frequently devoted to a single crop such as grapes or olives, or simply left uncultivated by absentee landlords. The single crop estates mean that armies of peasants are employed only at harvest-time and survive as best they can throughout the rest of the year. The estates left uncultivated rob the peasants of even this seasonal employment. By and large, too many of the big aristocratic landowners milk their estates of whatever provides money with least bother, and use that money to buy stocks and shares, tourist real estate, or else yachts and sports cars. This, unfortunately, fails to plough back into the countryside the money taken out of it, and is reflected in low productivity, inadequate mechanisation and antiquated methods.

The large estates have been a target for social reformers for two centuries now. From 1900 onwards a palliative was sought in the form of irrigation to improve agricultural yield. With the advent of the Second Republic a start was at last made on land reform, or confiscation of the estates and distribution to the land-hungry peasants, but this ceased in the turbulence of the Civil War being replaced by a system of irrigation and development of land for settlement, at high cost to the taxpayer, and which tends merely to nibble at the edge of the problem. The Republic's figures of 1931 showed that the ninety-nine Spanish Grandees alone owned nearly a million and a half acres, and the agricultural census of 1962 showed how little the picture had changed, for 0.8 per cent of the landowners still possessed 53 per cent of the registered land.

Politically less glaring, but none the less a grave problem, is that of *minifundio*, of tiny plots of land divided and subdivided by farmers for each of their sons for centuries, to produce the absurd situation of thirty-five million plots of less than two-and-a-half acres. As one farmer may own several plots scattered miles apart from one another, the time wasted in going from one plot to another, and the impossibility of applying farm machinery to such plots, all help to make this entirely anti-economic. However, much good work has gone into the solution of this problem, and a special land consolidation service of the Ministry of Agriculture has rationalised and concentrated holdings of four-and-a-half million acres since 1953. The cost has been high, but the goal worth while. A co-operative system of farming has also helped solve the *minifundio* problem, providing large areas for efficient cultivation with farm machinery. Despite the irrigation programme and the land consolidation, the agrarian problem comes back to the *latifundios*, a political matter, and the National Movement Minister and the Minister of Agriculture were still declaring in 1968 that *latifundios* failing to provide social solutions for the countryside would have to be expropriated. On the other hand, the peasants who remain are no longer so interested in owning their own small (anti-economic) plots of land as in enjoying higher regular wages and full social security benefits.

The most pressing needs in the Spanish countryside would appear to be tax penalties for the large estates left unproductive, flexible credits for the small farmer and capitalisation of farms on an industrial scale, together with training of manpower to operate farm machinery and rationalise cultivation. At present, the level of skills has improved only slightly from the 1965 figure

———

The Talgo (knucklebone) train, a revolutionary Spanish development.

Flag line Iberia, steadily expanding in South America, heavy summer commitment with the European tourist flow to Spain.

of an 84 per cent manual or semi-skilled labour force in farming. If tractors are the key to agricultural progress, Spain's total had risen to 190,000 in 1967 against the 58,000 of 1960, but the increase of 29,000 forecast for 1967 in fact amounted only to 23,000, a reflection of the high price of Spanish-produced tractors and the effects of the credit squeeze that year. There are now 22,300 harvesters. In addition, 900,000 acres have been irrigated since 1956.

It may be ironic that Spain's countryside is looking forward to a capitalist revolution rather than a socialist reform, but efficiency seems to point this way. Already the scarcity of able-bodied farm workers has sent wages up out of all recognition. Mechanisation is the inevitable next step, and this will demand capitalisation. If a sane commercialisation chain can be added as the third step, Spain's agricultural crisis could change to a new stage of profitable life, producing at home the meat and fodder now imported.

———

Valencia's Fallas, one mad night with nearly two hundred lath and plaster monsters going up in flames to ceaseless fireworks in a million-dollar bonfire. By day, a rival attraction to the beasts are the beauties, wearing the rich Levante-style dress, and hair arrangement vaguely reminiscent of the Lady of Elche.

G

CO-OPERATIVES

Spain has a large and potentially strong co-operative movement, though of the 14,000 registered co-ops with some two
million members, perhaps only 9,000 are genuine and active
ones, the remainder being commercial firms sailing under false
colours for tax reasons, or else moribund associations without
ambition or understanding of the co-op ideal. Two-thirds of the
genuine co-ops are agricultural, but their aim of providing cheap
food for the housewife and good prices for the producer has been
defrauded by the ramshackle and parasitic marketing system
they have not yet replaced. On the other hand, second and
third-stage co-ops, which handle distribution and selling directly,
could change this picture, and the large COES combine, a ' co-
op of co-ops ' which has received United States financial back-
ing ($35 million of feed-grain surplus for resale; ten-year, low-
interest repayment) can mark a breakthrough.

As it is, co-ops produce 24 per cent of Spanish wine, 36 per
cent of olive oil, 20 per cent of rice, 16 per cent of fruit and vegetables and 9 per cent of milk. They can all rely on State encour-
agement, often in the form of cash, as in the case of factories and
transport companies in which the workers take over a failing
concern and turn it into a co-op. Fishermen, consumers and
chemists also have their co-ops, if on a lesser scale, and while the
industrial ones may number only about 1,200 with 60,000 members, they include the remarkable Mondragon complex of factories and services.

Eleven years ago, the Mondragon co-ops did not exist. Today,
thanks to a remarkable priest, Fr Arizmendi, and a team of
devoted collaborators, this part of the Basque country has over
forty industrial, credit and consumer co-ops worth £15 ($36)
million, models of technical organisation as well as advanced co-
operative theory.

DEVELOPMENT

Spain's stabilisation of 1959 was followed in 1962 by the pub-
lication of a World Bank report on the Spanish economy which
was to be the basis of the First Development Plan 1964-67, a
scheme taking after French models and designed to be indicative
for private enterprise and binding for the ministries and public
companies. The Plan came in like a lion and went out like a
mouse, and its successor, the Second Plan, was postponed for re-
drafting at the start of 1968 while the calculators re-worked their
sums in the light of recent devaluation, the American investment
restrictions, and Spain's year of wage and dividend freeze. As
usual, the polemic surrounding the Plan (technocrats versus
Falangists) tended to obscure the facts. The vituperation greet-
ing its supposed failure was as unjustified as the triumphal drum-
beating which ushered it in.

The First Plan took stock of the realities of the Spanish economic situation. That is to say, it took stock of the fact that
there were no reliable statistics whatsoever about the Spanish
economic situation. It attempted to improve statistics, but inevitably, many of the Plan's calculations were thus flawed from
the start. It proposed a balanced advance on all fronts of 1 per
cent annually of the working population, and 5 per cent for productivity, the two to ensure a gross national product increase of
6 per cent annually. Heavy public investment was to finance
improvements in industrial equipment, mergers would be encouraged through ' concerted action' schemes for various sectors,
exports would be fomented, regional development would get
under way with expensive but necessary implanting of factories in
depressed areas. Thus Huelva and Burgos became Promotion
Poles; Vigo, La Coruña, Valladolid, Saragossa and Seville became Development Poles, with rounds of tenders held for firms
anxious to receive financial aids and tax advantages by installing
factories in these cities.

The aims of the Plan were ambitious but logical. Where
things tended to come unstuck was in the execution. The various

sector targets were missed or else exceeded with gay indifference, both by private and by public sectors, for the businessman in search of quick profits was not restrained by the Plan's indication, while the binding power on the public sector proved equally fictitious. The effect of public spending was inflationary, Spain's taxation system worsened its effects, and the flight from the countryside to cities was so much greater than expected that consumer demand bounded ahead while the shortcomings of agriculture were more brutally exposed. The outcome was the mini-stabilisation of November 1967 to check inflation born of galloping consumption.

In the subsequent recriminations, Plan opponents asserted that the scheme had been tried and found wanting, whereas the truth was rather that it had been wanted but not tried. For the Plan's targets had been set as reasonably as was possible in the jungle of Spanish economic statistics and organisation. But the planners at the Development Plan Bureau, though led by Señor Lopez Rodó, a powerful Minister, and with like-minded men in the other economics departments, in fact lacked executive power over the spending of the Administration as a whole, as also the power to indicate things strongly to private enterprise by knocking heads together. The planners and the *Sindicatos* (trade unions) were frequently at loggerheads, the former having inherited part of the latter's theoretical empire, and the lesson of the First Plan was perhaps that only a coherent Government under a forceful Premier could take planning out of the realm of wishful thinking.

THE LABOUR MARKET

The 1960s have been revolutionary for Spain, with the emphatic shift from agriculture to industry and services, from the rural interior provinces to the industry of Madrid and the north, and to the services of the tourist zones of the Mediterranean. According to the First Development Plan (1964-7), a steady but mild move along these lines would affect the 4.48

million in agriculture and fishery, adding them to the existing
4.02 in industry and the 3.67 in services. But the move became
a stampede, with the 1967 labour force of 12.56 million
divided into 3.75 in the primary, 4.6 in the secondary, and no
fewer than 4.21 in the tertiary sector.

Evolution of labour force by sectors of activity (per cent)

Years	Primary (Agriculture and Fishing)	Secondary (Industry)	Tertiary (Services)	Total
1900	61	14	26	100 (7,546,800)
1930	54	22	23	(8,772,500)
1950	49	25	26	(10,773,100)
1966	33	36	30	(12,201,800)

Distribution of labour force in Spain according to categories,
1965

Categories	per cent
Businessmen, managers, executives, experts and professional men	11.0
Employees (white collar)	10.5
Workers and self-employed	72.4
Services personnel	6.2
	100

Source : Instituto Nacional de Estadistica : Encuesta de pobla-
cion activa 1965 p 146

Spanish labour force, employed or self-employed

Kind of employment	1962 Absolute numbers	Proportion	1965 Absolute numbers	Proportion
Self-employed	4,281,317	36	4,302,617	35
Employed (wage and salary earners)	7,742,300	64	8,127,800	65
Total	12,023,617	100%	12,430,417	100%

Sources : Data elaborated from material of Ministerio de Trabajo
and Instituto Nacional de Estadistica

Recent global figures on occupations are not available, and in any case, statistics in this sphere vary according to official source, frequently by large margins. The breakdown derived from the 1960 census gave proportions of 3.6 per cent employers, 18.6 per cent self-employed, 65.7 per cent wage and salary earners and 12.1 per cent unpaid family workers. The ratio of men to women was about four-and-a-half to one—though higher in the employer and self-employed categories, and very much lower in the 'unpaid family worker' category, one to which all house-wives mentally add themselves. Jobs have changed so radically since 1960, however, that it would be pointless to quote the census findings, and instead, we may choose the National Institute of Statistics' percentage estimates for 1966, which suggest:

	per cent
Agriculture	33.3
Fishery	0.9
Mining and quarrying	1.3
Manufacturing	24.7
Construction	8.2
Electricity, gas and water	0.9
Commerce	11.6
Transport etc	4.8
Other services	14.3

Characteristics of Spanish employment are the low, though increasing numbers of women at work, and the relatively high proportion of the labour force under twenty years of age and over sixty-five, the former because of the short schooling offered, and the latter because of the inadequacy of retirement pensions as well as the practice of recording farmers as active statistically when no longer active physically. In the mid-60s about a fifth of the labour force was unskilled, though Ministry of Labour mobile training teams have made inroads into this problem since then with a scheme known as PPO, or workers' promotion, as an intensive supplement to existing vocational training facilities.

Evolution of categories in labour forces of Spain and United States, contrasting sub- and super-industrialised nations. Percentages

Categories	United States		Spain	
	1930	1950	1966	1971 (*estimate*)
Non-manual (industry and services)	29	37	28	37
Manual (industry and services)	49	52	38	37
Agriculture	21	12	34	26
Total labour force	100	100	100	100

Sources:

United States: Fritz Machlup *The Production and Distribution of Knowledge in the United States* (Princeton, N.J.: Princeton University Press 1962, p 382).

Spain: Data calculated from material of Ministerio de Trabajo, Instituto Nacional de Estadistica and Banco de Bilbao. (Note: Some professions resist precise classification.)

PAY

At the time of writing the basic minimum wage for all Spanish workers is 108 pesetas (13s, $1.56) per day, a rise of seventy-five per cent over the 60 pesetas daily of 1965. Whether the wages rose faster than the prices in the inflationary spiral of the mid-60s is a debated point. In 1967 some estimates put the year's average wage rises at 16.5 per cent. Naturally take-home pay was far higher than the minimum wage for all skilled workers, and the National Institute of Statistics classified bank clerks as the best paid workers at 72 pesetas an hour (9s, $1.08) and clothing trade workers as the worst at 21 pesetas an hour (2s 6d, 30 cts). The average for all workers was 31 pesetas, or nearly 4s (48 cts). Salaries are hard to determine in Spain, in view of the widespread concealment of true sources of income, but secretaries earn from £36 ($86.40) a month to £60 ($144), according to qualifications and knowledge of foreign languages. Executives from junior to senior status could rise from £60 ($144) to £240 ($576) a month, though at higher levels a variety of inducements and bonuses concealed from the taxman come into effect.

The great difference between the basic minimum wage and the take-home pay of most workers lies in the collective wage agreements concerted between the worker organisation and employers in most sectors, the three-yearly additional sums, incentives, and family points—the latter a fund provided by the employers and shared out by married workers according to the number of their offspring. During the boom years overtime was common in Spain, indeed excessive. This reflected managements' reluctance to engage more workers for whom fairly heavy social security quotas would have to be paid, and whom it would be hard to sack in later times of crisis because of Spain's 'no strikes, no sackings' rule. As a result the existing labour force at a factory was used for whatever degree of overtime circumstances demanded.

WORKING CONDITIONS AND HOLIDAYS

Spain's workers are in theory protected by elaborate rules on conditions, pay and hygiene, administered by the Ministry of Labour, but in fact there are too few inspectors to ensure compliance in small workshops and in the countryside, where workers can be victimised in many ways if they complain at infractions of the law. The bureaucratic nature of the Syndical Organisation appears to impede flexible response to these situations and ready defence of the workers. On the other hand, the larger firms are often better organised for worker welfare, and run medical services and leisure activities, in some cases even building minor townships to house their employees and educate their children. Bonus payments on 18 July (to mark the Nationalist rising of 1936) and at Christmas can be the equivalent of a month's pay, according to the agreements prevailing in that industry. Summer paid holidays vary from two to four weeks, with August worked in offices and factories on a token staff basis.

In addition, there are about fourteen religious feast-days in Spain observed as full holidays, when all work ceases. Half of these are later recuperated by an extra hour's work a day over the following weeks. Shops and some offices still work on Saturday afternoons, and there is no early closing day during the week. By and large, Spaniards still work six days a week. The official working week is forty-eight hours, or eight hours a day. But in fact, most Spaniards have to work longer hours to make ends meet. The FOESSA report on Madrid shows that while in the USA the normal working week consists of 40.3 hours, and in England of 45.9 hours, in Madrid it amounts to 51 hours. A quarter of Madrid's labour force is away from home at least thirteen hours a day. Many fathers see their children only on Sundays, because they are off to work before the children are awake and the children are asleep by the time they get back. Family life is the prime victim of two of Spain's most marked features, over-employment and pluri-employment.

EMPLOYMENT

1966 figures estimated that four and a half million workers, over a third of the labour force, held down more than one job. Recent university graduates and white-collar workers sometimes hold down three jobs, jobs badly served because badly paid. The Spaniard's aim is not one of loyal service to a particular firm in which he can rise, carving himself a satisfying career, but laterally, into as many different jobs as possible. Prosperity through skimping jobs and doing without sleep replaces promotion through merit. But pluri-employment and overtime financed all those television sets and cars during the consumer boom.

The employment situation becomes still more complicated in the countryside, where owner-farmers may work unlimited hours, but where hired workers suffer complete seasonal unemployment, especially in the *latifundio* regions of Andalucia and Extremadura. A FOESSA enquiry into a representative group revealed that in the countryside, 18 per cent were unemployed, 24 per cent were underemployed, and 34 per cent were overemployed. Industry registered 6, 7 and 42 per cent in these categories.

The Spanish Government's policy has always been one of full employment, but economic circumstances have dented this on occasions like the 1959 stabilisation plan and the November 1967 devaluation and austerity programme, which may not have been called a stabilisation plan but closely resembled one in its effects, which included a rise in registered unemployment from 170,000 to 217,000, and in estimated real unemployment from 250,000 to 325,000.

The credit squeeze preceding the 1967 devaluation had already reduced credits to firms in an effort to halt inflation, and the result was a list of bankruptcies and some 2,000 *expedientes de crisis*, near-bankruptcy applications whereby, with Ministry of Labour approval (not always granted), firms could declare workers redundant. Some 20,000 workers lost their jobs in this way, some of them receiving large indemnifications. But with unemployment allowances totally unrelated to living costs, the need to survive drives Spaniards into odd combinations of jobs. Army officers may work in the Syndical Organisation in the afternoon or else sell television sets. Taxi-drivers may be waiters in the evening and night-watchmen even after that. The effect of tiredness on their driving is visible next day. Even manual workers, who tend to do overtime on their factory job rather than seek a second one, suffer the effects, among which must be listed the horrific total of over 1,800,000 work accidents yearly.

ACCIDENTS AT WORK

The accident totals include those travelling to and from work, but they remain appallingly high in comparison with Britain's 300,000 for nearly twice the population and five times the industry. The Ministry of Labour runs a big 'Work Safe' campaign, but comes up against the tiredness we have mentioned, indifference to safety rules, Iberian bravado, and sheer *dumm-kopf* carelessness. The construction industry is outstanding amid this shedding of limbs, for it adds inexperience and low educational level among its workers to the unavoidable perils of height and the avoidable perils of engineering miscalculations of materials' strength. With a death a day in construction, a building permit is Spain's equivalent of the 007 licence.

PURCHASING POWER

This Spanish tendency to work too much (or rather too long, which is not necessarily the same thing), is neither frivolity nor just material greed so much as the need to survive in a rapidly-changing economic context. With cost of living increases of around 10 per cent a year throughout the 60s, Spanish prices are now lower than European prices only in certain spheres, mainly in services rather than goods, though the 1967 devaluation helped to correct this trend for the benefit of tourists. But while prices may approach the European level, purchasing power does not. One would like to know rather more about the way statistics like the following are compiled, but it was a fairly current belief in Spain that in early 1968 a Spaniard had to work 1 hour 5 minutes to buy a dozen eggs, against 10 to 13 minutes for the USA and Britain. A litre of milk cost the Spaniard 17 minutes against 6 and 9 minutes in the USA and Britain. A refrigerator meant 358 hours 14 minutes against 80 and 90 in the other two countries, while a car involved the unfortunate Spaniard in 2,682 hours against the American 666 and the British 960. A more recent comparative table based on 28 consumption goods —17 of personal use and 11 services—calculated that a Spaniard had to work 3,711 hours against an American's 927 and a Briton's 1,281 hours. This may sound discouraging, but compared with Spain's earlier economic situation it represents a striking advance, because formerly Spaniards could never hope for such consumer goods in their entire lives.

WOMEN

Legally speaking, women in Spain tend to be well-protected objects, objects with rights attached to them and transmissible to their offspring, but not greatly to be enjoyed by the women themselves, who require their husbands' permission for more or less everything. Spanish society is not kind to the lone woman, for it assumes that a woman must be either a wife, a mother, a daughter, a nun or an unpaid spinster home-help. Spanish male chivalry extends to all women unless they are defenceless.

Progress for women in recent years has come politically thanks to the Women's Division of the National Movement, under Pilar Primo de Rivera, sister of the Falange founder Jose Antonio. The devoted band around her are, to some extent, the Spanish suffragette movement, but with wider aims, which extend to several social spheres and preserve regional folklore with their Choirs and Dances Groups, while organising social service for all Spanish girls as an equivalent of their brothers' military service. Spanish girls cannot obtain passports or driving licences until they have done their social service, in courses at social service centres or in the form of welfare work. The courses bring together aristocrats and peasants in an effort, probably forlorn, to overcome distances and break down ignorance on both sides. However, this political rôle for women has helped in improving their working possibilities, and a quarter of the labour force is now female; about 3 million.

Further economic development, if allied to more effective taxation, will almost certainly increase the number of women at work, and possibly even earn them liberation from the restraints of their families' control. If that is what Spanish women desire, of course.

THE PROFESSIONS

The professions are a worthy, immensely dignified, and wholly uncharted aspect of Spanish society. Each profession, doctors, architects, lawyers and the rest, has its provincial college, culminating in a central, national one. The colleges are responsible for the registration of the new members, and ensure the observance of professional etiquette, while acting as an organ of professional defence—chivvying clients dilatory about paying the fees they owe, writing to the press and exercising other, discreeter activities to protect the professional image. A comforting blend of club and fortress to sustain professional men in their tasks, men whose earnings are one of the profounder secrets of their calling.

Thanks to Spain's corporative system of representation, the central colleges and institutes of professional men select trusty members to sit in the Cortes.

THE TRADE UNIONS

Spain's trade unions are not in fact trade unions, but *sindicatos,* 'vertical' syndicates which in theory combine workers and management in co-operation for the economic good of the nation, instead of allowing them their 'horizontal' associations which confront each other with the opposed interests of labour and capital. Similar German and Italian organisations in the thirties served as models for this Spanish State syndicalism, which outlaws any attempt on the part of the workers to form their own exclusive organisation with or without specific political allegiance (harking back to the powerful Spanish Socialist UGT before the Civil War, or the Anarchist CNT). Membership of the *Sindicatos* is automatic and obligatory for all Spanish wage-earners and employers.

The mammoth Spanish Syndical Organisation is in fact a department of the National Movement (basically Falange), and the movement Minister is at the time of writing also Syndical Head, though a formal division of the two posts is possible in the future. This will not affect the political tinge of the Syndical Organisation, however, as the 15,600 permanent staff in the 'command' chain are mostly Falangists. Imbued with fairly radical political ideals and with a built-in hostility to capitalism, which it would like to replace with extensive nationalisation of the banks, electricity and other main sectors of industry, the State Syndical Organisation is a force in the land, with property worth £37 ($88.8) million and a declared 1968 budget of £27 ($64.8) million.

Spanish business responds to the Syndical Organisation's verbal hostility with accusations that the bureaucratic slowness of the apparatus provokes more industrial discontent than it solves, while Spanish labour appears to view the organisation as a form of Governmental control rather than a means of worker representation. On the other hand, at factory level, the shop stewards and factory committee members elected in 1966 were unquestionably fairly elected representatives, and many of them still remain in their posts, if others have been dismissed since by the organisation. Though Spain is a member of the International Labour Office in Geneva, the peculiar character of the Syndical Organisation prevents this from being affiliated to any of the international trade union groupings.

Starting at shop-floor level, Spain's syndicalism provides for elected *enlaces* or shop stewards, one for every twenty-five workers. Firms with more than a hundred workers have joint management-labour committees, on which the employers (economic section), the workers (social section) and technicians are equally represented. These committees deal with wage claims, hours and working conditions, hygiene and other aspects to be included in ' collective agreements,' normally valid for two years. As Spanish workers do not enjoy the right to strike (till very recently all strikes were actually classified as subversion, with stiff penalties), there is little pressure that can be applied to the management representatives. On the other hand, more sophisticated techniques such as canteen boycotts, sit-downs, low-yield and the like have been developed of late, which can hardly be dealt with by the police but which certainly influence the management.

Each firm is included in a national syndicate grouping every unit in a specific sphere of economic undertaking; thus the Metal Manufacturing Syndicate; Mining; Cork and Timber, to name

only a few of the thirty national syndicates. Each of these syndicates operates at national, provincial and local levels, with its
management, worker and technician sections, which in turn
combine the workers' and employers' representatives from the
different syndicates in provincial, and finally a national Workers'
Council and a Management Council. The two main elements
combine once more in a general Syndical Congress. At the time
of writing a revision of the Syndical Organisation is under way,
in the light of suggestions made by the grass-roots elements.
Some of the bolder elements asked for an organisation in which
workers and employers were finally divorced, which was independent of the National Movement and the State, and in which
the important jobs were all elective and representative of the
workers, instead of the actual situation in which the occupants
of key posts are all named from above by the Minister
responsible. However, it was not thought likely that changes in
organisation would be allowed radically to alter the centre of
power in the Syndicates.

The Syndicates Headquarters, dependent on the National
Movement Ministry, has four main branches, one handling the
social or workers' side, one handling the employers' or economic
side, one dealing with administration, and the fourth handling a
small empire of welfare bodies such as the Housing Undertaking,
the Education and Leisure, Crafts, Health and Co-operatives.
These mainly duplicate the efforts of direct State organisations,
such as the Housing Institute and the Institute of Social
Security.

Headquarters runs the syndicates throughout the country
through the ' command ' line of officers, who consider the suggestions made by the economic and social sections, authorise their
meetings, approve or otherwise their agenda and so forth, attend
and chair the gatherings and ensure that all goes as planned. As
the foundation charter of the system put it, the Syndical Organisation is a unit in the service of the State. As such, the Syndicates
nominate trusted representatives to the syndical third share of
seats in the Cortes, on provincial and city authority boards etc.

The concentration into thirty major syndicates is an excellent thing in that it abolishes the futile demarcation disputes common in countries where dozens of semi-rival, semi-overlapping craft unions have members in one and the same factory. Many political sectors hostile to the present complexion of the Syndicates would wish to preserve the strong and simple lines of organisation. Whether the organisation could survive divisive tendencies of a political character—Socialist, Catholic, Communist unionism— is another matter. Even without the classic pre-war unions, sur- viving in latent and clandestine fashion, and a number of newer groupings with a strong Catholic left-wing contribution, the Syndical Organisation finds itself challenged by the *comisiones obreras* (workers' commissions), militant nuclei with considerable influence in the industrial cities, which organise strikes, demonstra- tions and other action to seek wage improvements and the right to organise freely. These organisations, avoiding political com- mitment on the surface, despite their harassment by the police, place the State Syndicates in a difficult position by showing up their inability to match radical words with radical action— strikes—as the Syndicates were created specifically to arbitrate between management and labour, so making strikes unnecessary (as well as illegal).

At the same time the Syndicates are threatened from the

Seville Fair, the most aristocratic, intoxicatingly gay event in Spain's full *fiesta* calendar. By day, horsemen and their trophies, by night, the never-ending dance of the *sevillanas*. Ending at four each morning for a week, Spanish cities live their fairs to the full, abdicating from work for the duration.

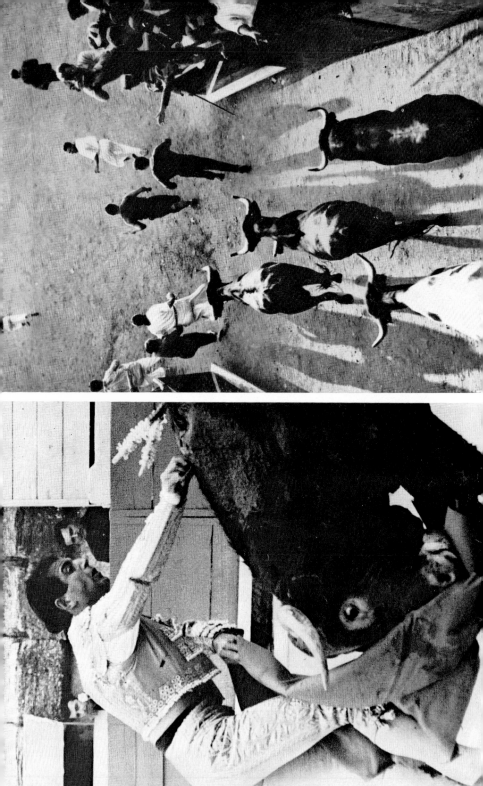

management side, as the younger businessmen want to be able to declare redundancies freely when the market so dictates. But free sacking would mean freedom to strike if a balance of power is to be kept. And freedom to strike would end the rôle of the Syndicates, for these could hardly initiate strike action, at least in the present Spanish political context.

As it is, any disputes which are not settled within the Syndical Organisation can be taken to the Labour Courts, which depend on the Ministry of Labour. These dealt with thirty thousand cases in the last quarter of 1967 alone, with an informal rapidity and efficacy which contrasts with normal litigation in Spain. It is more usual for these courts to find in favour of a worker than against him—reflecting perhaps the fact that only individuals with a good case are likely to press it so far. The usual cases in this sphere concern wages and overtime claims, work accidents and holiday rights.

However, when a large sector of an industry finds itself at loggerheads with management over something like a new collective work agreement, or when *comisiones obreras* leaders have been arrested, then strike action is likely to be launched and the Labour Courts are left aside. Spain has had its period for strikes, even since the Civil War, though these formerly never achieved

––––––––

Pamplona's San Fermin junketings are the most incredible wine-soused, blood-boltered performances, sprinting just ahead of the bulls into the ring. (Bull's breath on the kidneys is said to be a sovereign remedy for rheumatism of the legs.) The difference between the three escort *mansos* and the fighting bull is visible even from this angle. The neck muscles tell all.

The moment of truth, executed by a grand master, Antonio Ordoñez.

H

a mention in the censored press. Strikes in 1956 helped to end the official fixing of wages and ushered in the era of collective bargaining. Strikes in the mining valleys of Asturias in 1962 and 1964 also jolted the Syndical bureaucracy. In recent years strikes have been tolerated *de facto*, if not *de jure*, and are mentioned freely in the press. As a result they no longer seem so important as when they were surrounded with drama and prohibition. They have even dropped in frequency—from 777 in 1963 to a mere 179 in 1966, unless official statistics have been allotted the rôle of safeguarding public opinion once entrusted to official censorship (strikes were allowed to rocket up statistically in 1967 once more).

ALLOWANCES AND PENSIONS

Unemployment allowances and pensions for Spain's workers are part of the unified social security system described in Chapter 4, provided by the National Institute of Social Security or by Mutual Societies, and paid for by the workers and their employers, not by the State, which is to say, not by the taxpaying nation as a whole. The monthly quota of 18.6 per cent of each worker's basic wage (14.27 per cent paid by the firm, 4.33 per cent paid by the worker) is sent automatically by firms to the Social Security Institute. Of the total 18.6 per cent, 3.55 per cent goes towards funding family allowances, 3.05 per cent towards old age and invalid pensions, 8.4 per cent for health insurance, 1 per cent for unemployment insurance, 0.8 per cent for vocational training institutions, and 1.8 per cent is the Syndical quota.

The sums available for each kind of allowance therefore depend on the amounts contributed. This causes some dissatisfaction among contributors, who regard the quotas as deferred wages and ask why the workers should pay for their labour universities and vocational training institutes when the State meets the cost of the higher education available mainly to the upper classes. The Labour Mutuals operate a similar worker-employer system of monthly contributions, which can vary from case to case, but normally draws 3 per cent of the basic wage from the worker and 5 per cent from the employer. The self-employed pay 9.5 per cent a month themselves of a sum between 1,000 and 10,000 pesetas (£6 to £60, $14.4 to $144) at which they assess their monthly earnings. The Mutuals can offer a more flexible range of aid and allowance measures to their members than the social security system proper.

The disadvantage of Spanish unemployment allowances, shared with the other benefits, is that they are related to the *basic* wage of each rank of labour, ranging from the thirteen shillings a day of the unskilled worker to the £36 or $86.40 monthly of the engineer or executive, amounts totally unrelated to real earnings. This reduces the contribution, but it also reduces the allowances received if unemployment should strike, which are but 75 per cent of the *basic* wage plus family grants received before involuntary loss of job. Not everybody can claim the allowance therefore, which is restricted to those who have been contributing to the scheme for at least six months of the eighteen prior to loss of job. Benefits can be lost if the recipient fails to register at an unemployment office, refuses suitable jobs or refuses to take a re-training course without valid reason. The allowance continues for twelve months maximum, and the validity of medical cover during this period depends on the length of time the individual has been contributing to the scheme. The unemployed without rights to the allowance can get aid from the Work Protection Fund, furnished by the tax on stock exchange deals and worth £14 ($33.6) million in 1968, which helps in re-training, internal migration and the like. Though useful, this is a palliative rather than a solution.

Work accidents and professional illnesses draw small lump sum compensations if temporary and pensions if serious and permanent, with the sums ranging from 35 per cent to 100 per cent of the wage formerly earned. The amounts are brought more into line with present-day price and wage levels every so many years.

EMIGRATION

Like the Irish and the Italians, Spaniards have flocked across the Atlantic, though heading naturally for their own culture and language, as well as opportunities, in Central and South America. Two-and-a-half million since 1900 is the estimate, a million and a half to Argentina, 350,000 to Brazil (Galicians understand Portuguese almost better than Castilian) 225,000 to Venezuela and 100,000 to Cuba. Galicians in Argentina and Asturians in Cuba became finance and pressure groups of great power. English-speaking nations have received some Spaniards too, the USA 42,250 (including several thousand Basque shepherds), Canada 15,000 and Australia 12,000. Down under, the fertility of Spanish women and the skill of Spanish tennis players are alike much appreciated. However, many hundred thousand emigrants return to Spain at the end of their lives, some as poor as they went, others rich and eager to buy up their native villages.

The really dramatic emigration wave has of late been to Europe, though temporary circumstances drew 350,000 Spaniards to French farms as early as 1914-18. The defeat of the Spanish Republic in 1939 sent 528,000 political refugees across the border, many to die in atrocious French camps, others to join the Foreign Legion, fighting at Narvik and under Montgomery in the desert, or giving bite to the French *maquis*. By 1951 less than half the Spanish colony in France could still be described as refugees, and the purely economic factor dominated almost entirely by the end of that decade. Passportless frontier-jumpers were then replaced by a wave of legal worker emigrants fleeing Spanish unemployment under the 1959 stabilisation plan.

These were mostly aided by a specially-formed Emigration Institute, through which the Spanish Government protected its emigrant citizens abroad with documents and contracts and agreements of social security concerted with the host authorities. This spared Spanish workers the fate of Portugal's clandestine emigrants, exploited by the worst kind of European employers because of their lack of valid work documents.

Throughout the 60s the factories of France, Germany and Switzerland have provided the escape valve for over a hundred thousand new Spanish workers a year, in a ratio of three men to each woman, who stay abroad to survive, or if possible save, for periods of two to four years. In many cases separated from their families and sending home every penny earned, the stress has been severe, especially for peasants meeting foreign languages and foul weather alongside their first contact with city life. However, the single men and the united emigrant families with all members working have been able to enter the European affluent society, save money, and dazzle their native villages each summer in Opel or Peugeot—as tourists.

The actual number of Spaniards in Europe is hard to tell; a grand total of 1,150,000 includes 838,000 for France, at least half of whom should be regarded as permanent residents, not emigrant workers. The 1967 figures of 135,000 for Germany, 80,000 for Switzerland, 37,800 for Belgium and 25,000 for Britain are probably accurate. As it happens, 1967, coinciding with recession in Germany, marked the start of a reverse process, with more workers returning from Europe than going. That Madrid housewives need no longer phone Frankfurt for the plumber is small consolation compared with the alarm in Spanish official circles at the thought of a massive return of Spanish workers from abroad, not notably receptive to European political systems perhaps, but certainly accustomed to tougher worker-management bargaining than they would be likely to find at home. As 1968 recorded an unusual rise in unemployment, the return would cause a serious labour problem in Spain and, worse still, deprive the country's balance of payments of the workers' remittances, which for several years now have run at more than £180 ($432) million annually.

6

How They Learn

SPANISH education, all given in Castilian, is highly centralised in the Ministry of Education and Science, if we except farm schools run by Agriculture, fishery and navigation centres run by Commerce, vocational training and polytechnics run largely by Labour and the *Sindicatos*. Local authorities contribute only minimal sums to education and even these are frequently in arrears. Of primary and higher education, 80 per cent is supplied directly by the State, but only 20 per cent of secondary education. To a very large extent rigid bureaucratic control is harmful to quality, while the statistical vacuum leads to unrealistic planning. As a result, costly anti-illiteracy campaigns are mounted to redeem adults, while half a million to a million (nobody knows which) children are without compulsory primary education from the sixth to the fourteenth birthday.

True, illiteracy is now down to about 5 per cent of the population from the 17 per cent of 1950, while pupils at all stages of education have doubled in the last decade, and in secondary and higher education may do so again over the next five years. Evidently a considerable effort has been launched by the State since 1959 (the date in which Spain began to emerge from stagnation) but if the contrast between what exists and what used to exist is gratifying, the contrast between what exists and what should exist is still alarming. However, the new Education Minister (1968), Villar Palasí, has launched a revolutionary re-examination and re-organisation of the education system—freely admitting the bad things described in this chapter, and undertaking to change them with the aid of a Spanish and international brains-trust of educators.

Children at school and numbers of school-age children

Type of Education	Ages	Numbers at school (per 1,000 in age group) Academic years		
		1960–1	1963–4	1965–6
Primary	4–13	560	564	630
Education certificate (Bachillerato)	10–17	160	220	282
Secondary—vocational	14–17	92	107	134
Intermediate technical and Higher Education (both Technical and Humanities)	17–24	38	50	55
Total:	4–24	407	437	558

Source: Elaboration of data from Ministerio de Educacion y Ciencia and Instituto Nacional de Estadistica.

Studies in the mid-60s revealed that only 2.4 per cent of Spain's national income went on education (and 60 per cent of this was met by family economies), lowest percentage in Europe, and a mere half of the British percentage. The £4 ($9.60) per capita expenditure this represented at the time was but an eighth of the British per capita spending on education and a sixteenth of the Swedish, to mention the top European nation. Admittedly Spain was not then a developed country, and the education budget has since quadrupled, but, as the experts realise, development follows education.

Hence the concern in the newly liberalised Spanish press and the newly independent minority of Cortes Members when the 1968 Budget showed education expenditure virtually marking time with regard to 1967, despite annual cost rises of about 11 per cent in this field. In the Budget, 10.3 per cent of the total went to the Ministry of Education and Science, though the addition of sums from other departments with a stake in training brought it to 11.6 per cent, worth 27,758 million pesetas

(£166,500,000, $398,000,000). The Finance Ministry's Red Book on the Budget gives the breakdown as follows:

	pesetas	*per cent*
Education	27,758 m.	100
Gen. admin.	703	2.5
Research	469	1.7
Teaching	26,246	94.5
Primary	14,525	52.3
Vocational	1,783	6.4
Secondary	5,179	18.6
Technical	1,645	5.9
University	2,293	8.2
Special	821	2.9
Dining rooms, etc	340	1.2

However, the Cortes Members pointed to the million children without school places, the inadequate pay for State primary teachers, the minimal amount spent on scientific research, whereby Spain has 2 researchers per 10,000 of the labour force, against the USA's 36, and spends $1 per capita against the USA's $110, the outcome being an annual bill of £60 ($144) million for use of foreign patents. The Press and Cortes Members also drew attention to the minimal opportunities for the children of workers and the lower middle class to obtain higher education (between 6 per cent and 7 per cent, which is better than the demagogic 2 per cent widely quoted but grossly insufficient in view of the 66 per cent of the census composed of these classes). The £14 ($33.6) million available in PIO (Equal Opportunities) scholarships can but scratch at the surface of this problem, which resides in the 80 per cent share in secondary education of fee-paying private secondary schools. Of higher education students 5 per cent and of secondary 10 per cent receive grants. As workers' children mostly fail to get secondary education, they lack the standards to enter universities even if their parents could support them for so many years, which of course they cannot. The need in poor homes for every mouth to earn its own bread as soon as possible militates against educational advancement and ensures a high percentage of drop-outs even from primary education, where available. A pilot scheme of wage-grants for poor students to overcome this problem for a thousand pupils a year was announced with fanfares in mid-1968, applicable in higher education.

PRIMARY EDUCATION

As only 1 Spanish child in 4 receives infant education from 2 to 5 years, primary education from 6 to 14 (raised from 6 to 11 in 1964-5) is the key to the educational system. In 1968 some 4 million children were registered, a slight improvement on the 1965-6 academic year (the last with detailed figures), when 2,784,000 were taught in the 82,500 free State classrooms, 750,000 in the 17,300 fee-paying classrooms of religious orders, and 407,000 in the equally fee-paying 10,700 classrooms of private though non-religious-run schools.

Education and texts are free in the State primary schools, whose pupils return home for meals as a matter of course (there are some dining halls with 16-peseta lunches, partly mitigated by PIO grants), and these schools are served by 100,000 *maestros nacionales* who start at £30 ($72) a month and side-step into industry or commerce if possible. Some 32 per cent of the State primaries with 77 per cent of the pupils are village-type single classroom schools where one teacher copes with all ages and streams simultaneously, though experiments are being made with multiple-class regional schools with pupils transported in from distant villages. Many of these village schools have been left with vacant places by the demographic shift of two-three million people in a decade, while city schools are correspondingly overcrowded. In May 1968 parents queued for three days and nights outside a new Seville primary school to register their children; the city lacks 75,000 places. Ironically, while the number of children not receiving education, or dropping out from it, is between the (optimistic) number of half a million and the (pessimistic) one million, there are half a million unused primary school places in other parts of the country.

The First Development Plan made a valiant stab at this shortage, deducing a deficit of 27,000 classrooms and aiming to build 14,000 in four years. In fact, about 10,000 seem to have been built, while replacements and demographic growth, as studied by the DATA research firm, would indicate a problem increasing more swiftly than the solutions attempted, leaving a deficit of 25,000 to 29,000 classrooms in 1968, the building of which would take half the entire Ministry of Education budget for the year.

The Spanish child who enters the educational system finds himself processed inexorably year by year, *curso* by *curso,* each with its examination, the passing of which determines entry into the next course. Thus the slow can fall behind but the bright cannot skip ahead. At the age of six the child starts primary education, with four year-long courses which take him to the age of ten. This is where parental affluence begins to make itself felt, for the middle-class child can then enter secondary education with four year-long courses of *Bachillerato Elemental* or elementary education certificate in a fee-paying school, whereas the working and lower middle-class child can only aspire to one of the excellent (in many cases) State secondary schools, which are hopelessly few and far between. Failing this, the alternative is another four years of more advanced primary education till the fourteenth birthday (or in fact, often beyond it). A brilliant child of fourteen in the primary system can in fact then change over to secondary, if scholarships make this possible, but he will find himself at fourteen in course 3 of the elementary education certificate alongside children of twelve—an immense disadvantage. Thus primary education does not lead naturally into secondary.

For the great mass of primary school pupils, the future means unskilled labour. However, for the rich or lucky, the system involves the four years (ten to fourteen years of age) of the elementary education certificate, followed for about half the pupils by the two of higher certificate, and the one year, from the sixteenth birthday onwards, of ' pre-university.' The successful passing of the pre-university examination entitles the candidate to enter any university. This is the élite. Others who have obtained their elementary certificate may not aspire to the heights, but side-step into intermediate level technical education, which will make them assistant engineers and the like.

For the primary pupils whose parents cannot support them in secondary and higher education there is the alternative of vocational training, seven years starting at the age of twelve, which at its highest levels in the Labour Universities is the equivalent of the technical stream in secondary education, and at lower levels produces skilled technicians and mechanics up to the foreman category. This branch of education is heavily subsidised by the State, Church and other organisations, and places little strain on domestic economies.

SECONDARY EDUCATION

In March 1968 Spain had just over a million children and young people studying for the *Bachillerato* in its higher or elementary categories, and the addition of those involved in the ' entry ' stage plus others in technical and teachers' secondary studies brings the total to around 1,400,000. This is double the number in 1960, and if the Second Development Plan's previsions were to be fulfilled (which for reasons of bricks and mortar and provision of qualified teaching staff is unlikely), another 620,000 places would be created in the elementary stage (covering 60 per cent of the children from ten to fourteen years of age), and another 200,000 places in higher grade and pre-university course by 1971.

In the mid-60s only 17 per cent of secondary education was given in the State's *Institutos,* 35 per cent in recognised Church schools, 16 per cent in lay recognised schools (recognition depending on a certain level of staffing and attainment) and 32 per cent in *libre* or free schools and academies. The ' free ' in this case does not mean gratis, but free of State control; free pupils study at commercial crammers or on their own, but take their exams at the State *Institutos*. Apart from the annual *curso* tests, these exams include the *revalidas* after four and six *cursos* respectively which award or withhold elementary and higher *bachillerato* or education certificates. Streaming into science or arts subjects starts at fourteen after the elementary certificate has been obtained.

The State's small percentage of secondary education offers tuition free of charge, though there are other extra expenses to be met by parents. The religious order and private lay schools charge monthly fees that can vary from £6 ($14.4) to £30 ($72) for day boys with an extra £15 ($36) to £18 ($43.2) in the case of boarders. The top price range is naturally for an élite, and these schools are frequently found to be Jesuit-run. While the law requires private schools to provide scholarships for 5-10 per cent of their pupils, the top colleges make sure that these stay within the middle class. A conference of religious educators in 1967 called on the State to provide 20 per cent of its budget for education, and appealed for the 'democratisation' of education, which some observers understood to be a demand for public subsidy for private education.

Certainly, despite all the tax and rates exemptions granted to schools often occupying costly city-centre real estate, private education costs the State less per pupil than does the creation of new places in State-run secondary schools. On the other hand, only a drive to increase the number of State schools will help 'democratisation' in the commonly understood sense of the word. This is more important than ever, as the lesser religious and private schools face grave financial trouble and in some cases offer low-grade education. This is especially the case in girls' education, as nuns are cheaper to employ than lay teachers, but too often lack adequate educational qualifications. Furthermore, hours tend to be wasted with padding like embroidery (though not cooking). On the other hand, the university degree required of State secondary teachers is excessive, at least for the teaching of elementary certificate classes.

Save in rural areas, co-education is rare in schools, and girls leave the more old-fashioned convents with ideas on sex that are peculiar, to say the least. On the other hand, the text-books have been purged to a considerable extent of bigotry over the last ten years, and the Catholic religion texts, like gymnasium and 'National Spirit' compulsory unless parents specifically request exclusion from religion classes, no longer reveal quite such political-religious intransigence on the question of religious freedom, while the simplicities of ideology have been mitigated. History contains the patriotic exaggerations and whitewashings to be found in school texts all over the world, and rather carefully halts with the dictatorship of Primo de Rivera—before the controversial 1931 Second Republic. By general consent, the lack of mathematics and science teachers of sufficient calibre is a grave problem, and one which perpetuates itself.

Study at home continues, but homework in the form of exercises has gone, to be packed into the general 8 to 6 o'clock school day (9 to 6 if the pupil does not attend Mass). This long day contains a morning break of half an hour, and a lunch break of two hours. Free afternoons are Saturday and either Wednesday or Thursday. Sport consists mostly of kicking a football around the playground, or else more organised basketball. The latter is about the only practical activity in view of the lack of playing fields. However, more attention is being paid to sport nowadays, with athletics and swimming, as well as the soccer and basketball school leagues played with verve on Sundays. Holidays are long in summer, for obvious climatic reasons, and include all July, August and September, except in the case of State primary schools, which restart in September. In addition, there are generally fifteen to twenty days at Christmas and ten at Easter, not to mention all the national and religious feast days, which are a pleasant bonus.

There is no physical punishment in Spanish schools, although one assumes that the occasional clout or board-rubber is released in moments of maximum provocation. Discipline is maintained by force of personality, backed by the threat of writing out fifty or a hundred lines of 'I must not . . .' or else the withdrawal of privileges. Reports tend to deal with the behaviour of children rather than their academic prowess or capacities and potentialities; after all 'education' in Spanish means 'good manners.' While primary school teaching is a career for self-sacrificing women to whom secretarial and other jobs do not appeal, the disadvantages of women primary teachers outnumbering the men by almost two to one is now starting to be felt as twelve to fourteen-year-old boys stay on at school and require the sterner presence of men.

TECHNICAL AND SPECIALISED EDUCATION

This aspect of secondary education covers a wide field, and is generally for those who possess elementary or higher education certificates but do not anticipate continuing towards university. The numbers in each case increase by about a thousand students per year, but the detailed breakdown for the 1964-5 course is fully representative. It reveals just under 6,000 medical technical assistants, a quarter of them qualifying each year. In the 147 primary school teacher training colleges (two-thirds of them Church or privately run), combining the 'entry' with the full study-course pupils, we find just over 80,000, of whom 9,000 or so qualify every year. From 64 Seminaries 755 priests were ordained in 1964-5, from 24,300 students (a proportion reflecting not just the drop-out numbers, but the fact that seminarists can enter at eleven years of age). Lower arts and crafts schools had 14,000 pupils, and lower grade music studies had 19,000.

Vocational training schools, designed to produce skilled workmen up to master tradesman or foreman level, numbered 441, a quarter of them State-run, a quarter belonging to the *Sindicatos*, and the remainder private, Church- or Army-run. Of the 117,000 pupils in 1964-5, over 11,000 completed the Skilled stage, and 2,600 the more advanced Master stage. The complete cycle can occupy a youth from his twelfth to his eighteenth birthday. The vocational aspect is only part of the technical and general education given at the remarkable Labour Universities, a species of mammoth polytechnic with mainly boarding pupils, grant-holding sons of workers. There are twelve of them, starting with the enormous Gijon pioneer of the system, and most recently Valencia, to give a total of 25,000 pupils.

The Labour Universities are paid for directly by the workers from their pension funds accumulated by the Mutual Societies, and the first ones cost them £18 ($43.2) million to build, though the Gijon giant looks as if it must have cost that much by itself, and in days when pesetas were worth twice as much as today.

Proportion of grant-holders from total number of students in various levels of education, 1965-6

Type of education	per cent	Total numbers
Bachillerato	9	(834,290)
Teacher Training	6	(86,411)
Technical, intermediate level	4	(62,428)
Medical assistants	2	(6,379)
University	4	(92,983)
Higher Technical Colleges	4	(32,896)

Sources: Comisaria de Proteccion Escolar y Asistencia Social: Boletin Informativo (Madrid, March 1965), No 22. Instituto Nacional de Estadistica, 'Anuario Estadistico de España, 1968,' p 306, and following.

Evolution of numbers of grant-holders in higher education
Proportion of grant-holding students of total students

Academic year	University	Technical Colleges (Higher and Intermediate)	Total
1958–9	1.7% (62,895)	1.9% (27,489)	1.8% (90,384)
1961–2	2.2% (64,010)	2.8% (62,849)	2.5% (126,859)
1963–4	4.1% (80,074)	4.7% (75,070)	4.4% (155,144)
1965–6	4.1% (92,983)	4.6% (95,324)	4.2% (188,307)

Source: Comisaria de Proteccion Escolar y Asistencia Social.

Members of the Banking and Stock Exchange Mutuality recently pointed out that they had contributed 150 million pesetas to the Labour Universities, and that 208 of their sons had studied there, making it 720,000 or so pesetas a head. Expensive by any standards. Meanwhile the State budget paid for almost all the building and tuition costs of higher education, to which few workers' sons had access. Though no reliable figures are available as to the cost-per-place of different kinds of education in Spain, it is thought that university matriculation fee of £36 ($86.40) contrasts unfavourably with the £126 ($302) to £204 ($489) annual cost of keeping a boy at a Labour University. The Mutual Societies are anxious to hand the Labour Universities over to the Ministry of Education without delay, as this Ministry at present even fails to acknowledge some of the diplomas awarded by the L.Us.

The Labour Universities also teach what used to be known as the Labour Certificate, now converted into the Technical Certificate, which shares normal elementary education till the age of fourteen, and then divides off from higher certificate into technical subjects. The number of centres teaching this came to a total of 265 in 1964–5, exactly half of them Church-run, with 44,500 pupils, 5,300 of them finishing their studies that year. Commercial schools had about 20,000 pupils that year, just under 3,000 of them finishing their studies at two levels.

———

Manuel de Falla, intense, withdrawn. A small output of concentrated, perfected music.

The philosopher Unamuno, portrayed by Vazquez Diaz. The writer flung himself into every literary form with the recklessness he employed in political polemics.

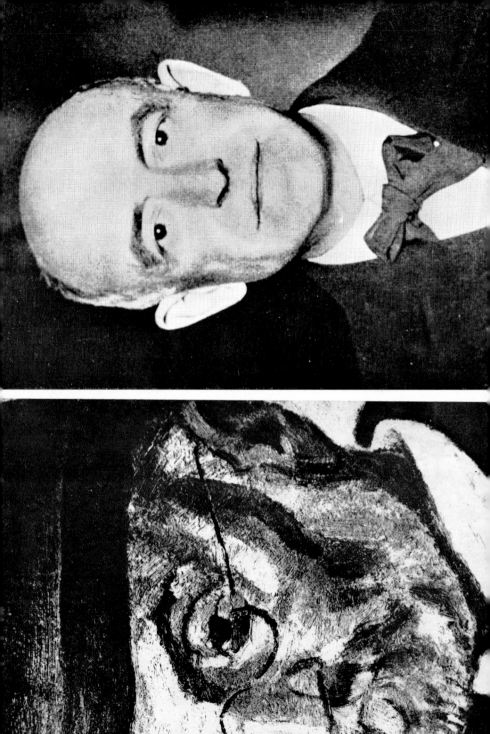

An important sector of education is the one covered by 52 Technical Secondary Schools, with more than 61,000 students, half of them preparing to be industrial technical engineers and the remainder builders, mining experts and the like. The 3,000 teachers managed to produce 5,250 students who had finished their studies in 1964–5. In that year, incidentally, these experts were still known as *peritos*, which sounds like a little dog trotting along obediently behind mandarins such as full engineers or architects. The title of technical engineer sounds more dignified, but the intrinsic disadvantages remain; namely that these schools are not part and parcel of the higher technical colleges. Were the cycles unified, those without the intellectual or financial ability to continue on to the highest levels would simply emerge younger as technical engineers, while the brightest or richest continued up the steep slope to full engineerhood.

As it happens, many of these technical engineers, builders etc in fact draw up the plans which are signed, as the law demands, by full engineers or architects. The same class-determined paper-qualification barrier also prevents many excellent accountants or business experts from reaching the positions their merits warrant. This situation has been described as highly indicative of an under-developed country. A further indication is the fact

---

Genius in art capturing magnanimity in war. Las Lanzas; Velazquez commemorates the surrender of Breda to the Spanish forces. At the Prado in Madrid, alongside countless master-pieces of the Spanish school and formidable collections of Italian and Flemish art.

' If it stirs, shoot it.' Spain is a great place for guns.

that while Spain's technical education hardly surpasses higher education in numbers of students, the OECD norm is eight times as many in technical as in higher.

However, recent measures have clearly attempted to link up the educational chain so that pupils can progress onwards and upwards without lateral hops into wholly distinct systems, probably losing a year or two in the process. Thus higher technical certificate plus the 'maturity proof' year and exam (technical equivalent of 'pre-university' year and test) gives access to university faculties and higher technical colleges, while the technical certificate without the extra year qualifies for entry to the technical secondaries.

HIGHER EDUCATION

At the time of writing, Spain's higher education, 80 per cent of it State-run, is administered through twelve university districts, based on the universities of Madrid, Barcelona, Santiago, Salamanca, Seville, Granada, Valladolid, Saragossa, Oviedo, Valencia, Murcia and La Laguna (Canary Islands). These universities are all of the Napoleonic variety, that is to say vast degree-providing educational abattoirs open to all with the appropriate educational qualifications who have the money and the patience to survive five year-long courses as a minimum. Those who fail a course merely stay on until they pass it, which creates a goodly group of students long in tooth and short in temper, especially in view of the insufficient number of jobs awaiting graduates. The drop-out rate is tremendous, however, and this saves the lecture halls from bursting at the seams instead of just swelling as at present. Only the nine species of higher technical colleges (from industrial to architecture, from telecommunications to textiles) have strict selection processes. This keeps their numbers down to 32,000 or so, while the university faculties proper now contain around 90,000 students.

However, there is no question of even distribution around the university districts. Madrid alone has 35 per cent of the total, and Barcelona 15 per cent. That leaves the remaining half for the provincial universities and technical colleges (very few). Admittedly, the university-town atmosphere of Santiago, Granada and above all Salamanca (heroic founder with Bologna, Paris and Oxford of Europe's college-based universities) produces a fairly concentrated student life absent in the big cities, but these lesser universities can never counteract the fatal attraction of Madrid and Barcelona for one very simple reason—they do not offer the full range of technical colleges or faculties.

The higher technical colleges have a fairly high rate of students completing their studies, thanks to their rigorous selection at the start. But the panorama is highly depressing in the university faculties. There are perhaps another two thousand students in each faculty in the 1967–8 course, but the pass-to-student ratio has not changed appreciably since 1964–5, when of 19,500 in the Faculty of Science 1,161 obtained degrees; Politics and Economics, 11,000 students, 345 degrees; Law, 14,750 students, 1,116 degrees; Pharmacy, 4,600 students, 514 degrees; Philosophy and Letters, 14,800 students, 1,018 degrees; Medicine, 19,750 students, 1,600 degrees; Veterinary, 531 students, 35 degrees.

Evolution of students registered and graduated in higher education

Academic year	Registered Science and Technical	Others	Total
1960–1	33,967	43,156	77,123
1962–3	39,352	49,000	88,352
1964–5	52,204	60,443	112,647
1966–7	65,700	73,600	139,300

Academic year	Graduated Science and Technical	Others	Total
1960–1	1,838	3,405	5,243
1962–3	2,258	3,588	5,846
1964–5	3,348	4,086	7,434
1966–7	4,800	5,800	10,600

Notes:

Scientific and technical education includes: Physics, Chemistry, Geology, Biology, Exact Sciences, Pharmacy, Veterinary, Engineering and Architecture.

Others include: Medicine, Law, Philosophy and Letters, Politics and Economics.

These figures also show the odd selection of university subjects, with vets and chemists on their own while all Arts subjects are lumped into one faculty, Philosophy and Letters and all Science into another. To explain to some degree the fail or drop-out rate in Economics, it should be mentioned that most students take this as an interesting extra discipline for a few years, while studying Law or Philosophy and Letters as their degree subjects. Likewise, many register initially in Science before passing over to the higher technical colleges (which, incidentally, have higher social cachet). The number of students in higher education has gone from about 37,000 in 1940 to around 140,000 in 1967. The joke has it that in Spain only ' sons of good family ' could formerly attain university degrees, whereas today, ' daughters of good family' can join them. About a quarter of the students are now girls, rising to 60 per cent in Philosophy and Letters, but dropping to 2 per cent in higher technical colleges. Estimates of foreigners, mainly South Americans, oscillate between 9,000 and 14,000.

The problems of the Spanish university are broadly: too many students for the present installations, with absence of personal contact between teachers and taught; under-utilisation of the installations that do exist, which could probably cope with the present numbers if used in three shifts; rigid civil service administration and lack of university autonomy; chaotic syllabuses determined by 1,000 or so senior professors, who are lords and masters of all they survey. Though the numbers of assistants and lecturers has been increased in recent years, the professor continues to dominate the system. Each Chair is won in competitive examination and thereafter held for life. Consequently the occupant cannot be sacked, even for the grossest neglect of his duties. And this is what tends to happen in too many cases.

Not all, but over-many *catedraticos* regard their professorships merely as a boost to their status and fees in their private practice of law, medicine or whatever; this hardly leaves them time to stray near their classes at the university, which either wait in vain or else have a few pages of the obligatory text-book read at them by an underpaid junior assistant. This text-book will probably have been written by the professor himself and sold in instalments at a high price thanks to the fact that he alone examines and awards course-passes, and eventually degrees, as the whim takes him. The Spanish professor is the intellectual equivalent of the absentee feudal landowner, who in this case extorts toll from those forced to pass that way.

To sum up the various ills of Spanish education which find their culmination in higher education, we may say that primary is for the workers, secondary elementary for the lower-middle and middle classes, secondary higher for the middle and upper classes, and higher education for the upper middle and upper classes. The State has not yet made secondary education available to the nation at large, and this blocks off higher education for the lower classes. In addition to the insufficient quantity, the quality is highly suspect, as teachers are forced to take too many jobs at the lower levels and choose to take too many jobs at university level. As a result, pupils spend too many years on each stage of their education and are forced to cope with frequently changing syllabuses surmounted by rote-learning of prescribed texts. The regurgitation-type of education destroys capability for original thought without preparing the victim effectively for a career, as the texts are not notably modern or adapted to career realities.

This sombre picture is alleviated however by some non-State initiatives such as the Opus Dei university at Pamplona, which pays for a proper teaching staff and sees that the students are taught. Learning from the Oxbridge and American systems equally, Pamplona has shown what university autonomy with a serious concern for pedagogy could mean. However, only religious organisations (the Jesuit university at Bilbao-Deusto, the Pontifical at Salamanca) can seriously rival the State system, for purely financial reasons. Fiercely criticised by many professors as a university for the élite, Pamplona's greatest sin in their eyes is probably that it shows what can be done, with the onus on educators to get on with their own job rather than sitting back and blaming the State.

There is reason for hope that the additional universities for Madrid, Barcelona and Bilbao (with further faculties for Santander and neglected Extremadura), announced in May 1968, denote a breakthrough for greater autonomy and efficiency in Spanish higher education. If the system is presently in crisis, this merely brings it in line with Spanish society as a whole, struggling to emerge as a denizen of the industrialised West. Solutions can be found, and concretely on the educational front, problems are being tackled with energy by the present Education Minister Villar Palasí, who started by raising an additional £42 ($100) million for his new universities and faculties.

However, student life in Spain seems curiously lacking in the companionable, gregarious element common in Britain and the States, while failing to produce any recognisably Left Bank substitute. Sports facilities exist at university level, but about the only facility much used is the faculty bar. The university colleges are glorified student hostels, and the 162 all over the country (44 for women) can cater for about a tenth of the student population. All-in costs at these can be as low as £15 ($36) a month rising to as much as £36 ($86) in the most luxurious. Scholarships, already rare, are inadequate for residence at all but the cheapest colleges, in the unlikely prospect that these have places available. Questioning of 1,334 girl students revealed that only nine relied entirely on their scholarships, while 1,193 were supported entirely by their families. The remainder combined scholarships with either part-time work or family support.

For the poor student, the solution is shared rooms in some grubby digs. Possibly the university riots which have become an ever more constant feature of Madrid academic life are an attempt to compensate the lack of gregariousness noted above, as well as the need for some kind of competitive sport, plus a way to keep warm in winter.

7

How They Get About

GETTING about has long been one of Spain's greatest problems, and the mountain ranges that resist road and rail, yielding grudgingly to mules, have greatly hampered the economy. If we except the river Guadalquivir which takes small coasting ships up from the Atlantic to Seville, waterways are mostly non-navigable, save by canoes. There is a much-discussed plan to cut a deep canal from Seville to Bonanza on the coast, but the cost has so far left it on the shelf with ideas for a tunnel under or a bridge across the Straits of Gibraltar.

Spain's economic recovery plans in the 40s laid more emphasis on production than on distribution, and by the 50s transport had become a major problem—the railways slow and inefficient, internal air links far from developed, the roads bad and the haulage fleet antiquated. Even in 1960 filling stations were rare oases. Since then, however, the picture has changed radically, road surfaces and layout approximating to most European standards, if still far short of American. All highways have their filling stations, and these are now spreading to secondary roads, receiving their fuel—96 the top octane—from the Campsa monopoly organisation. The improvement has been motivated largely by a wish to satisfy tourists and attract more, but the Spanish car boom of the 60s also made it unavoidable.

RAIL

Spain's railways have increased their ton and passenger per mile ratio in the 60s, though at only a fraction of the road haulage improvement rate. With the exception of 2,800 miles of local, narrow-gauge track belonging in some cases to the State, in some cases to private companies, Spain's main network of 8,200 miles in wide gauge (5.5 ft) is run by the RENFE, as the nationalised railway company is known from its initials. Over-staffed, and except for the upper echelons, underpaid, the RENFE is the target of public grumbles justified by the odd places people have to go to collect tickets, tickets carrying a complex series of surcharges for 'speed,' a quality more evident on the ticket than on the track. With a 1966 turnover of £93 ($223) million, the deficit was £22 ($52.8) million. It is hoped to break even by the 70s.

The RENFE inherited trouble from its creation in 1941, which was a great relief to the previously existing private companies, whose track and rolling stock had been decimated by the Civil War. This destruction was one more blow for companies which had been formed from 1840 onwards, largely with foreign capi-tal, to run a railway system on the cheap, using light rail incap-able of sustaining fast heavy traffic. And admittedly the terrain was no help, with only 22 per cent of Spain's track absolutely horizontal, and 66 per cent without curves; 4,000 bridges, 1,165 tunnels and nearly 16,000 crossings of various kinds had also to be negotiated by cautious locomotives.

Matching these disadvantages with Spain's general post-war lack of cash, it was not surprising that the railways lost business to road haulage. While in theory trains could carry more oranges to Europe, to mention one vital but perishable export, in practice the gauge change at the French frontier made this uneconomical. However, an adaptor to the *Talgo* train now makes it possible for these Spanish trains to reach Paris and Geneva, with a new service due to start in the summer of 1969.

The paucity of Spain's railway network by comparison with other European countries may prove an advantage as modern concepts of rail traffic are introduced, for the system is radial, with Madrid as centre of the octopus. There is little secondary traffic, and the Madrid to coast lines can be adapted for liner trains. Recently-cut tunnels under the capital now permit through traffic from north to south, and the new line laid from Madrid direct to Burgos in 1968 cuts two hours off the eight from the capital to the French frontier at Irun-Hendaye. Computerised signalling can overcome the disadvantages of so many stretches of single-track line.

The improvements form part of a ten-year modernisation plan launched in 1964, aiming to invest £422 ($1,012) million, £48 ($115) million of this coming from World Bank loans. By 1973 the present staff of 108,000 should be reduced to 79,000, and electrification should be widely extended. Meanwhile the electrified track amounts to 1,800 miles, with 600 electric locomotives and 776 diesels (far cheaper to run than steam) out of the total of 3,200.

Even today, not all Spanish trains are interminable chuggers with primitive carriages defenceless against extreme heat or cold. The TER and TAF trains are comfortable and reasonably fast, while the *Talgo* train, brought into service fifteen years ago, is one of the world's most interesting innovations. Designed by Goicoechea and developed by Oriol, the *Talgo* or knucklebone train is a low-slung articulated carriage with an original suspension system, which snakes along at speed and gives the sensation inside of a luxurious aircraft.

SEA

Over 80 per cent of Spain's foreign trade is seaborne, though the country's own merchant fleet of 2,000 ships with a gross registered tonnage of 2.2 million fails to avoid a deficit of over £50 ($120) million in shipping charters and transportation costs. Great efforts are being made to carry more goods in Spanish ships, and a flourishing shipbuilding industry supports the drive to achieve a tonnage of five million by 1975.

The oldest Spanish craft are the coasting tramps, which cannot rival road haulage, first, on account of age, but also because they fall under higher taxes and suffer excessive red tape and slow turn-rounds in Spanish ports, where only the first timid experiments in container-handling are under way. Sea links between the peninsula and the Spanish islands and North African possessions are handled by a monopoly company, which keeps fares low thanks to State subsidies, but does nothing to stimulate efficiency. The newer passenger ships are mainly devoted to pleasure cruises, as emigration to South America has fallen off sharply in the last ten years.

As happens in so many sectors of Spanish industry, the shipping firms are many and small, no fewer than 115 companies, 77 of which own a gross registered tonnage of less than 10,000. Several are in business with just one tramp, not to be overhauled until it sinks. The resulting under-capitalisation and inability to modernise hardly need stressing. There are some large companies, however, based mainly on Bilbao and Santander in the north, and they form a Central Maritime Office which used to distribute charters until freighting was liberalised in the 60s to produce a more competitive situation.

Spain's ports number 336, of which 10 are important, and the 1967 handling figures show 107 million tons of goods and 5.5 million passengers. Bilbao and Barcelona handle general traffic, Aviles and Gijon in the north handle coal and iron ore, Cartagena in the south takes in heavy quantities of crude oil for its refinery, Majorca and Malaga welcome tourists, while the Canary Island ports of Santa Cruz and Las Palmas are a pair of key fuelling stops for ships following the West African coast or crossing the South Atlantic. Both do extremely well whenever the Suez Canal is closed.

The Government has spent considerable sums on port improvements, though mainly to quays, breakwaters and on dredging. Goods handling equipment has lagged behind, while the administration leaves much to be desired. As a counterpart to its 1965 loan of £16.6 ($39.8) million for Spanish port modernisation, the World Bank demanded not only a raising of port tariffs but a reorganisation of administration in the direction of business efficiency and decentralisation. The tariff rise is likely.

AIR

Air transport is peculiarly suited to Spain, a large, under-populated country free of dense international air patterns, with difficult land communications. Commercial aviation in the penin-sula dates from 1919, but the major developments came with the creation of the State's Iberia Airlines in 1940, all of whose shares were transferred in 1943 to the National Institute of Industry. Iberia has a good safety record and draws on military pilots with many hours on their flight sheets and as often as not training in the United States to their credit. They are leased or released to the company by the Air Ministry, which also deals with civil aviation, and is mindful of Iberia's share of tourism traffic (2,630,000 out of 11,300,000 passengers in 1967); a modern version of downing the sword to bring in the harvest.

Iberia is phasing out piston-engined aircraft on all save the shortest flights, and by 1968 boasted 8 DC–8, 15 DC–9 and 19 Caravelle jets; it handles Spain's regular international flights, linking the main European capitals with New York and South America, via Madrid, and also running routes down the African West Coast. Internal routes are shared with the sister com-pany, Aviaco, and a pool is operated with the leading foreign airlines, most of which schedule stops in Madrid or Barcelona and the tourist resorts such as Majorca, Malaga and the Canary Islands. Of the forty-two Spanish airports, Majorca is the busiest, with a summer turn-round as busy as Berlin during the airlift; 2,727,000 passengers in 1967, marginally more than Madrid and well above Barcelona.

The fastest-developing phenomenon in aviation is the charter flight, of especial importance to a tourism country, and Iberia shares charters with foreign lines, as also with Spantax and Air Spain. Charters mean that Scandinavians can enjoy a fortnight in the Canary Islands, all-in, for about the same cost as the regular air passage on non-charter flights; a benefit not to be scorned.

ROADS

Save in Roman times and the brief reign of General Primo de Rivera, Spain's roads have never enjoyed great fame. One reason why speeding is an offence almost unknown in Spain is because road surfaces have effectively prevented it. However, a road revolution has been in progress over the last five years, and motoring is no longer the soul- and spring-destroying experience it used to be, one's car bounding from pothole to pothole. Road-mending is no more in the hands of gnarled and patched peasants tamping down the gaps with a hatful of pebbles as of yore. Instead, huge yellow machines lay down blankets of hot asphalt with a sigh, armies of smartly-overalled men marshal the traffic with walkie-talkies and wear construction-worker tin helmets, as if they were on bad terms with the jackdaws which cross the road in low volleys just in front of car wheels. As traffic is extremely slight except for the months of July and August and on Sundays near the cities, driving in Spain has become a joy, especially on secondary roads with lovely scenery and no rush.

The total network of roads amounts to 87,000 miles, but the essential arteries are the six National Highways fanning out from Madrid's Puerta del Sol—zero point. These wheel spokes carry 80 per cent of Spanish road traffic. The remainder is borne by regional, and finally by local roads, which are rather too widely meshed for efficient communications and are variable in quality. Spain has a mile of road to every 2.27 square miles of area, just under half the European average, while the mile per inhabitants ratio is also just under half the industrialised norm.

The problems to be overcome include awkward tracing of

road lines, for these were evolved to suit pack animals rather than coaches in the past, and are not the best kind of thing for modern high-speed traffic. A tremendous task of ironing out dips and curves is thus under way, and one trusts that adequate financing is laying sufficiently deep asphalt instead of the old five to nine inches, about a third of the depth needed for heavy traffic. Excuses which lay all the blame on winter snow and summer heat are no longer acceptable, and the press is now free to draw attention to shoddy contracting practices which formerly caused Spaniards to jest that road surfaces lasted just long enough for the builders to collect their money, but not a day more.

As always, Spain has a Plan for roads too, and it has a vast programme of flyovers and accessways, griddling the country with fast roads. To be completed within twelve years, and made urgent by Spanish traffic which doubled between 1962 and 1967 and the tourist bottlenecks along the Mediterranean coastline, this Plan contains 1,800 miles of high-speed, multi-lane *autopista* or motorway, at a cost of over £1,000 ($2,400) million.

The Government cannot charm such sums out of the air, so the building will be turned over to private enterprise, and the builders will operate the roads on a toll-basis for a fixed period, after which they will revert to the State. The savings in time and nerves will more than compensate the toll. Work has already started on short stretches linking the French Biscay frontier with the Spanish Basque coast, and also between Barcelona and the French Mediterranean border.

British and American drivers who would die rather than hoot a crude horn on the open road in Spain will probably die if they do not. In Spain you must hoot before overtaking, and quite apart from the rules, it is essential, for no Spanish driver has ever been known to look in a rear mirror, which is in any case obscured by a dangling dog or doll. The driver meanwhile is himself deep in solitary thought, or if accompanied, deep in discussion. Do not mistake his gesticulating arm out of the window as a traffic signal, he is just emphasising a point in the argument. As a result, his forward motion is slow and unaggressive, which makes overtaking him easy; it is the sudden lateral movements you have to hoot against.

Spanish truck drivers, one is constantly amazed to find, are the most careful and courteous in the world, and with an array of winking rear lights take positive joy in helping the motorist to get past on tricky stretches. It was not always so. They have been among the world's worst. The transformation was wrought by the formation of the *Guardia Civil* motor-cycle division, sea-green inflexibles that even Spaniards respect. Never cross that unbroken yellow centre line approaching a corner, never ignore the no-overtaking signs on a hill, for the *Guardia Civil* are watching and will get you for it. Argument is useless and the fine inevitable.

Many Spaniards wish they would also take over in the towns, where humble white-helmeted point-duty traffic police in blue, who have probably never touched a steering wheel in their lives, blow their whistles, windmill their arms under chic summer parasols, and are helpless amid the anarchy.

Our good opinion of truck drivers does not extend to rural bus drivers, the men who serve in hundreds of locally-contracted companies. There are more than 2,200 local bus routes in Spain, according to an admirable guide which shows that the peseta cost of a journey is generally two-thirds of the kilometre distance involved. Armed with the guide and a few words of Spanish, the enterprising can go virtually everywhere in Spain at low cost, if curiosity is placed higher than comfort.

CITY TRANSPORT

Transport in towns and cities means taxis for the foreigner, and Spanish taxis carry a green nightlight on their roof and a different coloured stripe or panel of paint in each city; thus Barcelona taxis look like wasps and Madrid ones have a maroon stripe. They are still cheap, and drivers are delighted to chat with anyone who can master enough Spanish, providing journalist visitors with the necessary quotes on the political and economic

situation ' from a generally well-informed source.' Some Spanish
and apparent familiarity with the city on the passenger's part
releases the driver from the moral obligation to indulge in false
détours, to the relief of all concerned; failing this, you should
just carry a Spanish newspaper. The taxi business is much less of
a closed shop than before, when licences changed hands at a high
price, and supply now matches demand. The rainy-day battles
to trap a taxi are mostly not-so-fond memories from the past.

Cycling is a sporting passion in Spain, but otherwise practised
only by those who cannot do better, from home to factory on
city outskirts, from village to fields in the country. And women,
never. Cycling in city centres is unknown for both sexes, and
women can appear only as passengers on scooters and motor-
cycles. This is more obviously provoking than if they rode the
contraptions themselves, but it provokes as women should pro-
voke, with their legs, not their independence.

How then does the city work force get to office or bench
in the morning—and home for lunch at half-past two, back to
work at five, and home again at eight, creating not so much as
a rush-hour as a rush-day? Public transport is perfectly adequate
in August when half the inhabitants are away. For the rest
of the year, Madrid and Barcelona offer surface and underground
transport. Above ground, the capital has single-decker buses (the
old second-hand London buses are out to grass, like the trams),
some of them double length and articulated; fifteen hundred
units which in 1967 moved 440 million passengers. In addition,
a series of spanking new mini-bus lines, farmed out to private
enterprise, fill the route, time and price gaps between regular
buses and taxis.

The Madrid Metro dates from 1919, and is still expanding,
though like a tortoise to the city's rabbit. Less fetid than the Paris,
nowhere near as clean and trim as the London, the Metro is
useful at all hours save rush hours, when the crush deals hardly
with ribs and wallets and people trapped in the ruck are carried
protesting several stations past their destination. Men always give
up their seats to old ladies, by the way. The Metro runs till
shortly after one o'clock in the morning (the buses continue to

two and more), and for two pesetas, or not quite threepence (three cents), one can go anywhere. The buses also charge the one price, irrespective of distance travelled.

All this is internal city travel, for commuting does not exist in Spain, save for workers in the suburbs (suburb is a pejorative word in Spanish) inadequately connected with the centre. Housing is vertical, in blocks seven to ten storeys high, so the physical area of towns never matches those in Britain or the United States. Only the extremely rich live just outside the city in houses with gardens. And of course the chief victim of Spanish non-commuting is the printing press. There are no regular, long, comfortable journeys to encourage reading.

CARS

'Spaniards drive like women,' so a taxi-driver told me, quoting with no enthusiasm the words of a visiting foreign journalist. One can see what he meant. A camera set up practically anywhere in the big cities would film a species of Mack Sennett script for tortoises. But if most Spaniards drive like novices, it is because most Spaniards are. Ten years ago only the Ministries, the millionaires and the bullfighters had cars. Admittedly Spain's motorisation is scant in absolute terms, and in relative ones boasts only 42 cars per 1,000 inhabitants against the United States' 393. But twenty years ago Spain had only 3 per 1,000. Vehicles doubled from 1962 to reach the 1967 figure of 3 million (1,250,000 motor-cycles and scooters, over 500,000 lorries, vans and buses, 1,230,000 cars), and will double again by 1970. What is more, most of them are packed into the handful of big cities, and Madrid alone passed the 700,000 mark in 1968.

The vehicle boom has been the most conspicuous element in the Spanish consumer revolution of the 60s and its symbol is the little Seat (Fiat manufactured under licence), which started modestly in 1950. At first, while cars were still rare and labour abundant, it was common to see uniformed chauffeurs and large dowagers crushed into a little Seat, rivalled only by the horde of official cars taking bureaucrats' wives to the hairdresser. (The official cars tended to be Cadillacs and Mercedes.) But before long cars were being produced in sufficient numbers to satisfy the queues awaiting them, the cost of second-hand cars actually dropped below that of new ones, more foreign firms set up factories, Chrysler buying 77 per cent of Barreiros and Britain entering with Morris and MG. With recession, 1967 saw the first stocks of unsold cars piling up, forcing the Government to think again about the heavy tax burden carried by Spanish vehicles, which means that a £400 ($960) car carries £80 ($192) tax. Comprehensive insurance for such a car comes to around £40 ($96), and for the rare imported foreign vehicles (which double their factory price before they get on the road in Spain), comprehensive insurance is prohibitive. Consequently, most Spanish cars make do with obligatory third party coverage, and rely on cheap garage labour to hammer out and repaint the damage caused in the course of the year, mainly to parked cars by children and by other cars trying to park.

Some sources estimate that spending on cars and motoring accounts for 5 per cent of Spain's national income and that the State garners nearly £200 ($480) million a year from vehicle and petrol taxes. Gasoline is by no means cheap, with 96 octane super at 11 pesetas the litre, about 6s 10d (80 cts) the gallon, and 98 octane, where available at 12 pesetas; 85 octane is cheaper, as of course are gas-oil and other industrial fuels. It is advisable to buy gasoline at busy city filling stations and if possible from the handful run directly by the Campsa monopoly.

Spain's insurance companies are becoming more sophisticated and also more uneasy as city traffic builds up and bumps and bangs proliferate. The 1966 accident total of 74,000, with 3,222 deaths is no cause for complacency, but the statistics should be explained a little. Even the mildest contretemps is classified as an accident for recording purposes, and the deaths are partly caused by the tourist rush in July and August of tired and irritable Central Europeans towards the sun and sea, when the foreign cars actually outnumber the Spanish.

K

By 1968 the city parking problem had entered a stage of crisis only partly solved by blue zones in central areas, with parking limited to an hour and a half. Commercial van loadings are supposed to take place only at fixed, tranquil hours of the day, but of course do not. Little space is left in residential areas, and half the fine old squares have been ripped up to install underground parking lots (being restored to historic appearance afterwards), and Madrid had 6,000 parking lot car spaces at the end of 1968, handling five times that number of cars in a day. The driver in the capital already pays a heavy city parking tax and is then preyed upon by the feared crane-truck, which hauls away the mildly ill-parked as well as the flagrantly. It was always more natural for the Spaniard to double park than just to park, but by now it has ceased to be a taste and has become a necessity.

Whenever the municipal finances are low, armies of traffic police march out to pop fine papers under windscreen wipers, aided by many wholly unreasonable no-parking signs on broad streets. However, the citizen matches unreasonableness with inviolable dignity, and being a Spaniard, and hence in the right, tears up the traffic tickets—3,000 of which are issued daily in Madrid, 80 per cent of them for parking offences. By the time the municipal pen-pushers have got round to processing the fine a year later, the offender has gone to Germany, or died, or the world has ended.

Driving schools sprang up like mushrooms—in some cases like toadstools—through the 60s, the instructors largely former lorry drivers because they had the most complete licences. The folkmyth is that in Spain nobody passes the driving test unless they come through a driving school (money must be made, after all), and that, especially coming through a driving school, nobody passes first time (for after all, somebody must continue to make money). Against this plausible belief we may place the Spaniard's psychological craving for conspiracies to explain his failure. The test itself is a characteristic piece of highly theoretical overkill, designed to pose a ferocious obstacle but in no way contributing to raise the level of national driving skill. Suffer first, revenge later, might be the learner's motto. There are hopes, with the transference of testing to the Central Traffic Department in 1968, that a more pragmatic system will be evolved. Meanwhile, one notes the apparently conflicting statistic that while 42 Spaniards in a thousand own a car, only 25 in a thousand own a driving licence. The rogue 17 per thousand seem to be the ones we always meet. Perhaps the contradiction is purely statistical, for alternative figures quoted 3,500,000 drivers by the end of 1967—only 7.5 per cent of them being women.

For while traffic in France is fast and perilous, and in Britain and the States is slow and relatively safe—in Spain the traffic is both slow *and* dangerous. A remarkable achievement, thanks to the surge of over-powered egos in under-powered cars. However, a few basic rules can take the danger out of city driving in Spain for the foreigner. The most essential are a) nothing can be taken for granted, and b) there is only one golden rule; biggest has right of way. Hints to complement these laws are that a flashing indicator does not indicate the direction in which the car is about to turn, but the direction from which it has just come. Cars waiting at traffic lights never register the change to green until the fifth in the queue hoots, but if Spaniards fail to start at the green they make up for this by not stopping at the red. Amber means accelerate, and a dozen circumstances can give the driver moral justification for crashing the red. Precisely this moral aspect moved the half-dozen drivers to get out and upbraid a Dutchman who had halted promptly on the red, causing all the following cars to ram each other and him. With only half the cars of other capitals, Madrid has twice the number of traffic lights, no doubt because the authorities rely on drivers to ignore half of them, probable in any case, as they are so badly placed as to be invisible when buses or trucks are around. Indeed, traffic lights correspond well to Spain's proliferation of laws-to-be-ignored, just as the traffic corresponds to the civic reality.

The traffic pattern, then, is one of ear-splitting scooter-vans, buses and taxis throwing out lethal clouds of black smoke, the latter less a form of transportation than class warfare transposed to four wheels, cars drifting across lanes relying on your warning hoot before contact occurs—forcing everybody to drive too close to the car in front in order to prevent intromissions. To sum up, the Spaniard at the wheel, while not aggressive, is the very model of mechanical incapacity, lack of civic spirit, obliviousness to the existence of others, as well as lack of interest in anticipating the shift of traffic patterns ahead.

There are yellow zebra crossings for pedestrians, which entitle the user to burial in sanctified ground, but the visiting driver should never employ courtesy, as this will inspire pedestrians or other drivers with the deepest suspicion, resenting a possible insult or probable mortal trap. But after so many unkind words, one must confess that Spanish reflexes are superb, or so much potential disaster could never produce so few collisions.

8

How They Amuse Themselves

SPANISH leisure divides into traditional and modern, and the two co-exist today, the former in villages and country towns, the latter a discovery of the big cities. Country leisure is the seven o'clock *paseo* or stroll on Sunday evening outside the village proper or in the main avenue of the town, girls together, boys together (save for the acknowledged couples or *novios*), all dressed to kill, all acting and reacting and studying each other under an air of furious unconcern. The *paseo* exists still in the cities, but with a high society and fashion-conscious air to it, and limited to a few streets lined with cafés with tables on the pavement for better study of the merchandise. The street is the true Spanish theatre.

The monotony of life in the *pueblo*, the village (now alleviated by television) is broken once or twice a year by a *fiesta*, a period of high spirits and much dancing, of soccer matches and funfairs, and, of course, a crude bullfight in the main square. At city level, these *fiestas* become something as sophisticated and magnificent as the Seville April Fair, the Valencia *Fallas* (with half a million poundsworth of fireworks and elaborate lath and plaster monsters burning in one night), and the Pamplona San Fermin bull-running. The wine flows freely, but the electricity of the atmosphere is most intoxicating of all. Each *barrio* or district of Madrid used to have its *verbena* or funfair, but these are slipping, and the San Isidro Fair each May consists almost entirely of sixteen bullfights.

Formerly, the professional classes of the cities would meet

for endless men-only political and other discussions in cafés, but now the cafés have been replaced by quick in-and-out cafeterias, and the men are at home watching TV or else driving the family out for a weekend picnic, enjoying the vehicle revolution. Off they go to the sea, the hills, lakes, or ski-slopes—the wonderful Pyrenees, or the ranges outside Madrid or Granada. Fishing in the fine salmon and trout rivers of Asturias draws many, and the shooting season is a perilous one, for Spaniards, mad-keen guns, are impelled to shoot everything that flies or stirs. However, the bag is not limited to pheasant, quail and partridge, but expands to include the handsome capra hispanica, a vast mountain goat, deer, and even wild boar and bear in the more rugged mountains.

The metropolises of Madrid and Barcelona have a very wide variety of urban diversions, whether taverns with rows of attractive *tapas* or snacks, luxury restaurants and interesting *tascas* or cheap restaurants (the former for the nouveau riche, the latter for the ancien riche). Young people are gaining ever greater freedom from parental control, and have innumerable discothèques for their entertainment. Night clubs and cabarets for adults also abound, but strip-tease is not permitted in Spain any more (at the time of writing) than is gambling. The latter taste is catered for by the State-run football pools (worth over £25 ($60) million a year, top prizes up to £400,000 ($960,000)), and the famous lottery. Dating from 1763, the lottery has draws every month or so, but the special summer and Christmas draws cause temporary madness, and Spain now spends more than £100 ($240) million on lottery tickets, Madrid accounting for almost a third of the total (the canny Catalans spend less but win as much).

Visitors find it odd that the last performances of films and plays should start at eleven o'clock at night, and that, especially in summer, the streets are more crowded at two in the morning than two in the afternoon. With more than 8,000 cinemas, Spain is second only to Italy in box-office takings in Europe, according to some estimates, with £30 ($72) million declared turnover in 1966, over half the entire declared Spanish entertainments turnover. As the declarations are for tax purposes, the real amount is perhaps twice or three times as much. By comparison, the theatre brought in only £4.4 ($10.56) million, cabarets £1.7 ($4), dance clubs £2.6 ($6.2) and 'various' £1.2 ($2.8) million.

Full summer heat in the cities drives people to the swimming-pools, and the *Sindicatos* have one in their recreation park to take a theoretical nine thousand Madrileños. Easter Week is a commercial blank, and Christmas lasts from December 24 till January 6, though not of course as a commercial blank. Many of the fourteen national holidays for major saints and the like can be linked to weekends by skipping the intervening Friday or Monday. And August as an active month simply does not exist; 300,000 people abandon Madrid on July 30, though many husbands sweat out the month at the office, rejoining the family in the mountains or on the coast at weekends and explaining away wife's suspicions as to their *Rodriguez* or grass-widower antics in the wicked city packed with Nordic visitors in mini-skirts. For office or factory workers, paid holidays range from two weeks to four, and of course there has been that welcome extra month's wage on July 18.

Middle-class Spaniards now tend to head south to the sun, hypnotised by tourist practice, instead of north to the cool, as formerly (the Government removes to San Sebastian). But estimates suggest that only 27 per cent of Spaniards, against the European norm of 50 to 75 per cent, leave home for holidays, and that only a quarter of these are workers—who head back to relatives in the *pueblo*. About 4.5 million cross the frontier every year, though to what extent they are tourists is debatable.

SPORT

Spain is actually becoming quite a sports-minded nation, though the propaganda to encourage this is still more abundant than installations to make it possible. A Sports Department of the National Movement has the job of boosting something which has hardly existed in Spanish schools, which have space only for basketball courts. The absence of sport (apart from obsessional kicking around of soccer balls) has been largely the outcome of absence of grass.

At university level all sports exist, from fencing to rugby, and Spain has made great advances in athletics and swimming, spurred by failure to win even one bronze medal at the 1964 Olympics. The 1967 Mediterranean Games told a different story. In the professional sphere, there are good boxers—Legra and Carrasco—and good cyclists who specialise in mountain climbs on the Tour of Spain as well as the Tour de France. The basket-ball teams are of international standard, notably Real Madrid (with several tall Americans). Burly Basques in the north row whalers and chop tree-trunks as amateurs, and as professionals indulge in *pelota* (or *jai alai*), slamming a hard ball over artillery distances against a wall with bat, accelerating basketsling or bare hand. Gilded youth sails, water-skis or goes in for motor racing on Madrid's new Jarama circuit. Gilded age watches the horses or golfs at clubs for millionaires, though the tourist is now catered for on the Costa del Sol.

Tennis has been the revelation of the last four years, thanks to the genius of 1966 Wimbledon champion Manuel Santana, who brought Spain triumph in the Davis Cup over every nation save Australia. However, all these are nothing by comparison with the Spanish passion for soccer. They jest about it, recognise it as a deliberately fomented substitute for political partisanship and passion, call it ' the Spaniard's ideological siesta,' but it is no jest. Defeat of the local team casts gloom upon a whole region. Supporters of *Atletico de Madrid* and triumphant *Real Madrid* are not on speaking terms after a game. *Real Madrid* usually wins the soccer league, and has been European club champion six times. Without question it is one of the greatest teams in soccer history. Spaniards are happiest to see it measured on the greensward with Manchester United, just as the Spanish national team has a tradition of matches against England. Characteristically, however, the individual Spanish clubs are always far better than the composite Spanish team.

Surprisingly, sport (basically soccer) was reputedly worth only £5 ($12) million or so at the turnstiles in 1966, somewhat less than the bullrings take for the year, though there are ten times as many football matches as bullfights. On the other hand, bullfight tickets cost ten times as much. Within these financial mysteries lies the certainty that the Spanish soccer aces are among the most highly-paid in the world.

THE BULLFIGHT

Above all, Spain is the land of the bullfight—the cricket and baseball equivalent—to the extent that it is the summer spectacle following winter football. The matadors calculate their triumphs according to the bulls' ears awarded them after each performance, and these are duly listed as their batting averages. Not quite cricket, nor quite baseball, for that matter. Either the foreigner likes bullfights or he doesn't, and I shall not argue for this or against. Everybody must go and see for himself. But most foreigners undoubtedly do thrill to the colour and skill of the *corrida*, and Spain's national spectacle would now be ailing but for the massive tourist public—and the erratic but compelling performance of El Cordobes, sometimes known as the Beatle of Bullfighting.

El Cordobes is technically mediocre, but his single-handed restoration of bullfighting in popular esteem is the outcome of a film-star personality amidst theatre actors. Generally speaking, the bullfight is a relation between man and wild animal in the ring, with the public as spectator. In the case of El Cordobes it is a relation between man and public, with the bull only too often as spectator. The rise from rags to riches of El Cordobes, illiterate labourer from Palma del Rio, satisfies a deeply-needed human emotion, and, remarkably, nobody seems to begrudge El Cordobes his eight cars, five farms, thousand head of cattle, hotel, block of apartments and private aircraft. Possibly because nobody really wants to earn money his way. Describing one of his worst gorings to this writer at lunch on his new estate (while guests dropped in casually by light aircraft) El Cordobes recalled the horror one afternoon at Granada, when he was caught and swung into the air like a doll, 'Somehow, that horn had jammed in my bones, in my pelvis, there I was, tossed up and around, pushing for all I was worth, *and I couldn't get off that horn*!'

Robbing a bank is a quicker and safer way to fortune than this spectacle variously described as sadistic butchery, the world's most visually beautiful religious rite, and a ballet in which one partner —the bull—cannot be rehearsed. A different race entirely from the domestic bull, the fighting bull is half a ton of slender legs, massive chest and neck, armed with stiletto-like horns with which it jabs like a boxer hooking. It is as fast as a racehorse over short distances, and can turn on a sixpence. In past centuries, one fighting bull killed a bear, a lion and a tiger successively, with only the latter proving a real problem. How can men survive with it in the ring? Thanks to the cape, which lures, guides and blinds the charging bull, not yet accustomed to man as enemy. The two-legged vertical line that is man can avoid the four-legged horizontal line that is bull, using the animal's impetus to carry it past safely.

Bullfighting as we know it was developed towards the end of the 18th century by Pedro Romero of Ronda, who took it over from mounted aristocrats and divided it into acts for skilled professionals on foot, elaborating the rules and also the style. What is more, he killed 5,600 bulls and suffered not a scratch, and those bulls were mature five- and even six-year-olds, not the artificially fattened three-year-olds of today, bumbling and falling around the ring, their weight far too much for their bone-structure.

Horn-shaving and doping are less current than under-age bulls, which save their breeders a year's feeding and care, and cost the public the same—about £2,000 ($4,800) for a string of six. The star matadors insist that peril shall be bred out of the animals, seeking as they do ' the small bull and large banknote.' The result is like a Grand Prix motor race with a 40 mph speed limit, but the breeders must comply or go out of business, unless they are real purists like the brand of Tulio and Isias Vazquez, near Seville, whose bulls are athletic five-year-olds trained like champions—and never to be found on the big-money festivals like the Seville Fair, or Madrid's sixteen *corrida* San Isidro May festivity. The matadors will never touch them.

To some extent they cannot afford to, not from fear of death, but fear of spending three weeks in hospital and so losing, say, ten fights. For bullfighting is commerce, worth millions a year in the world's five hundred bullrings, four hundred of which are in Spain (the rest in Mexico, South America and a few in France). El Cordobes and one or two more can command £12,000 ($28,800) for an afternoon's work, but the average matador must be content with about £400 ($960) to £600 ($1,440), 70 per cent of which goes automatically on expenses (manager, team, travel, accommodation, adverts, bribes to ' critics,' who, save a noble handful, are merely publicists for hire). Those not invited to the South American winter season, or not permanently on the string of fighters carried by the two or three big promoters, can suffer a precarious financial life to match a precarious physical one, with a body scarred and patched like a quilt, and only the bullfighter's patron saint, Sir Alexander Fleming, between them and death.

This sounds too negative. To understand what moved Hemingway to write bullfighting literature, Goya and Picasso to bullfighting art, one must hear the brazen sound of the *pasodoble*, witness the glittering parade of the bullfighters in their ' suit of lights,' and react with the alarm or admiration of the huge crowd as someone like Diego Puerta creates truly mobile sculpture from the ingredients of absolute valour, Andalucian grace and a flamboyant, baroque skill with the cape.

FLAMENCO

If bullfighting is one prong of the cultural assault launched on Spain by Andalucia in the last century, and by Spain on the rest of the world in this century, the other prong is flamenco dance and *cante* or song. Fine artists such as Antonio, Pilar

Lopez, Jose Greco and others have brought flamenco and Spanish regional dances to worldwide audiences with their touring companies. These give a false idea of the quality of 90 per cent of the flamenco on commercial offer to the tourist in Spain, which is banal verging on the atrocious. The exception is Madrid (not Andalucian cities), which draws the really talented performers, most of them gypsy, to half a dozen *tablaos* or clubs of high standards.

Here the performers sit in a half-circle facing the audience, a pair of guitarists with ulcered expression drawing filigree magic from their instruments, a couple of men singers in black suits and ruffed shirts—these expanding like sails as the powerful diaphragm fills, and then releases the complex oriental halftones of the *cante*. Lithe young men in ornate waistcoats, high-heeled boots and bolero jackets rattle their feet on the floorboards like machine-gun fire, and of course there are the half-dozen girls in close-bodiced, multi-coloured dresses that flare out at the hip into a mass of flounces and petticoats resembling a carnation—the carnation the girls all wear in their sleeked-back hair. A non-titillating spectacle, flamenco is none the less passionate, concentrating sex rather than exploiting and so dissipating it. Furthermore, in every *tablao* there is one girl who is the most beautiful you have ever seen.

The spectacle starts at eleven at night, continuing till two or three in the morning. The only comparison is a jazz jam session, though flamenco cannot evolve as does jazz. On the other hand, it has been taken over largely by the underdog (or possibly overdog) race of the gypsies, the *gitanos*. In Andalucia and wherever they settle, the gypsies burst spontaneously into flamenco at weddings and baptisms, dancing and singing *alegrias* and *bulerias*, and other light-hearted modes associated with the gay low-lying coastal regions—Cadiz, Seville, Huelva. This is *cante chico*. The *cante hondo*, deep or great song, is another matter, the blacksmith's *martinete*, with no guitar, but anvil accompaniment, the black *taranta* or miner's song, *soleares*, the melodic *caña*, *petenera* and *granaina* which have a Jewish rather than Arab air to them, these are the heart of flamenco. Nobody knows how it started, or what the word really means—apart from Flemish, which is an odd association for something so oriental, maybe because many gypsies accompanied the lavish retinue of Charles V and his Flemish courtiers when they first came to Spain. Perhaps it means simply flamboyant, or flaming. It is more enjoyable not to know.

MUSIC

There is little concert-going in Spain, for Spaniards by and large do not listen to music (Spaniards by and large do not listen). They do not listen to music because they are usually too busy making it, bursting into song and strumming upon the guitar with absolute spontaneity. Perhaps this is why Spanish classical music never strays far from this marvellously rich stratum of folk music, the *flamenco* of Andalucia, *sardana* of Catalonia, irresistible and athletic *jota* of Aragon, pipe and drum airs of the Basque country, plaintive Galician bagpipe music, gay *seguidillas* of Castile.

One likes to detect echoes of these even in the rich choral music of the late Middle Ages, the composers of the 18th century like Padre Soler, and of course, in the Chopin-inspired nationalism of the late 19th century keyboard composers, Albeniz and Granados, and the violinist Sarasate. Regional themes are also the staple fare of Spain's substitute-opera tradition, the *zarzuela*, a genre with a dozen brilliant composers rivalling the light opera of Vienna.

In the present century the ascetic Manuel de Falla evolved from the Andalucia of 'Love the Magician' through the Aragon of 'The Three-Cornered Hat' to the Castile of 'Master Peter's Puppet Show' and ended with the Catalan inspiration of 'Atlantida.' Turina's output was based essentially on Seville as theme, Guridi used Basque melodies (closely resembling Welsh and Russian choral music). More eclectic are the generation of Ernesto Halffter, Oscar Esplá and Joaquin Rodrigo, whose guitar 'Aranjuez Concerto' has achieved world-wide popularity.

Spain also boasts a modern school of composers, from the transitional Roberto Gerhard (who lives in Britain) to the advanced Luis de Pablo, Cristobal Halffter and Xavier Montsalvatge. Of the orchestras, the Spanish National can reach heights if conducted by young lions like Frühbeck de Burgos, and especially (on record, now, alas) by the late Ataulfo Argenta, a Toscanini of Spanish music. And only Spaniards can perform Spanish music—foreign musicians are invariably too sentimental, they miss the hardness, the rhythm.

Spanish sopranos include some of the world's greatest—Victoria de los Angeles, Pilar Lorengar, Teresa Berganza and Montserrat Caballé, while the Spanish guitar is an exclusive of this country, and more precisely of the great Andres Segovia, who single-handed (double-handed, perhaps) brought this neglected instrument into the concert-hall, whither he has been followed by Sainz de la Maza and Narciso Yepes. Pianists include the well-known Jose Iturbi and the incomparable Alicia de Larrocha, with several fine virtuosos in the younger generation, while Pau Casals is the giant of the cello, making this into a solo instrument much as Segovia did the guitar.

Barcelona has the only full opera season, at the Liceo theatre which Madrid now rivals with a State-sponsored May Festival. Oviedo in Asturias also has an opera festival, but the finest Spanish experiences in music are at the events with extraordinary visual settings—the Santander Festival in summer, the Cuenca religious music week at Easter, and above all, the Granada Festival, when one can hear Segovia play in the courtyards of the filigree Arab palace of the Alhambra, with Antonio's Spanish ballet in the Generalife gardens.

ART

Spain has always been a world power in painting, thanks to a towering genius or two per century—Greco in the 16th, Velazquez in the 17th, Goya in the 18th—rather than through schools of painters. The present century has if anything intensified Spain's artistic contribution, with the elegant tourist poster-style Valencian Sorolla at the turn of the century and the fashionable portraitist Zuloaga in later years as the home-consumption masters. However, the Spaniards who made their home in France for greater or lesser periods (acquiring the oxygen to match their Hispanic spark) are among the giants of our era. Picasso, Salvador Dalí and Joan Miró (Catalans by birth or in the case of Picasso by adoption) and Juan Gris, need no introduction here. It is interesting to speculate to what extent their imaginations were fired by the extraordinary *art nouveau* buildings left to Barcelona by the great architect Antonio Gaudí.

Painters less well known abroad, but highly regarded in Spain are, in the older generation, Daniel Vazquez Diaz, who uses cubism to strengthen his representational forms; Pancho Cossio, who dwells in partly representational studies with marine themes, misty as his beloved northern coasts, and Solana, a ' black ' artist whose satire goes beyond realism to achieve something like horror at the human condition.

Artists who have captured the sternness of Spanish landscape, the solidity of trees, starkness of vines in winter, immensity of skies, are Benjamin Palencia, perhaps the first *fauve* in Spanish painting, and a dynamic colourist; Ortega Muñoz, with his stylised devotion to the rock, the ploughed field, converting the natural into symbol, and the remarkable Rafael Zabaleta, an almost *naif* painter from Andalucia whose peasant figures are constructed architecturally, in angles and circles, against a schematic background.

Wherever the garde is most avant, a Spaniard will surely be found, whether in pictures of sacking and metallic scraps like Salvador Soria, or in sociological crowd-movements like those of Genoves. But more satisfying achievement in recent years has come through the work of groups—a rarity in this country. The Barcelona ' Dau al Set ' group of the 50s includes the widely praised Tapies, Cuixart and the miraculously luminous abstract colouring of Tharrats. In Madrid, the abstract artists include the subtle galaxies of Vicente Vela and the swirling, exploding forms of Manuel Viola, who will surely be commissioned as a battle-flight artist to record the first interplanetary wars.

A score of first prizes at recent international Art Biennales would show the Spaniards well ahead of the rest of the field. In many cases it is easier to read about such work than to actually find it, but it so happens that in the Modern Art Museum brilliantly installed in the strange old houses hanging over the gorge at Cuenca, much of the finest post-war work in Spain can be studied at leisure and with pleasure.

THEATRE

The Spanish theatre has a terrifyingly rich heritage of classics to live down—the 16th-century works of Lope, Calderon and Tirso. Nothing much happened from that moment until the present era. However, the first third of this century saw the charming Andalucian comedies of the Quintero brothers, the rural dramas and then the social comedies of Benavente, whose *Los intereses creados* is a minor classic, the blood-boltered poetic drama of Garcia Lorca—*Yerma, La casa de Bernarda Alba*, his prophetic epitaph of *Maria Pineda*, or the exquisite *La zapatera prodigiosa*. Today, even the ' barbarous ' plays of Valle-Inclan can overcome staging problems and censorship to appear, and they reveal a Theatre of the Grotesque, both sardonic and overpowering, as if Brecht were wedded to J. M. Synge. By contrast, the well-made ' poetic ' plays of Alejandro Casona wear less well.

Spain has a traditional talent for farce, and from Arniches at the turn of the century, through Muñoz Seca to the surrealist lunacy of Jardiel Poncela, this talent has blazed. It is sad that language barriers seem to cut off Spanish writers from the world scene, for Jardiel Poncela especially is a true innovator. Since the war, Miguel Mihura has best expressed this vein, which descends thereafter to the five-a-season potboilers to tickle the crassest bourgeois sentiments of the audience from Alfonso Paso, who most probably ' could do better if he tried.'

A realist school took shape in the 50s, left-wing and un-compromising in its social attitudes. Unfortunately, plays by Buero Vallejo, Alfonso Sastre and the more recent Lauro Olmo, to mention only three, are few and far between, for commercial as much as political reasons, for Brecht, Sartre and Soviet dramatists are now staged freely. Unlikely to be staged in his native country for some time, however, is the Spanish avant garde dramatist Arrabal, who shocks audiences in Paris, a genius very possibly, but one bad for the blood-pressure.

Spanish theatre is basically Madrid theatre, with twenty-three playhouses including the State *Teatro Nacional* for classics, *Maria Guerrero* for modern classics, and a sponsored experimental theatre. Barcelona has but half a dozen (some devoted to drama in Catalan), and the other cities depend on touring companies from Madrid, which tend to be second teams, as the best players cannot afford to leave the capital with its film and television perks. The middle-class comedy which is the staple diet (starting with housemaid on telephone) can be mounted for a mere £500 ($1,200), excluding cast wages, and will run from 100 to 300 shows, if highly successful, with performances at seven and eleven, six days a week. Houses will be two-thirds empty for all but a few plays, save at weekends, so no booking difficulties arise.

Acting and staging are frequently excellent, and actor-director Adolfo Marsillach's version of Arthur Miller's *After the Fall* was better than the Parisian version. The top half-dozen players and directors deserve international recognition but do not receive it. Critics who are both trenchant and impartial do not last long, so word of mouth rather than reviews brings success. A typical Madrid theatre year revealed 136 works staged, of which 68 were comedies, 29 dramas, 14 revues, 8 variety shows and 17 unclassified. The same year in Barcelona saw 28 companies stage 38 plays (7 per cent in Catalan), half being comedies.

Tribute must go to the many university and experimental drama groups who have prepared audiences and managements alike for plays by the more serious playwrights of the time.

L

FILMS

The Spanish film scene has long been a desert in which directors Bardem and Berlanga (who made together *Bienvenido Mr Marshall*) were the lone palm-trees. Few Spanish films between 1940 and 1962 have gained or merited showing abroad, being for the most part quota-destined pap made by fly-by-night companies for £50,000 ($120,000) or so, the cost being recouped by fiddling the books and claiming official subsidies even if the product never received screening. Children's films like *Marcelino, pan y vino* were sometimes distinguished and rather more adult than the work destined for the general public by a rigid and ludicrous censorship which had all acceptable foreign films dubbed into Spanish so that lovers could be turned into husbands, husbands into brothers, and which, fleeing adultery, often stumbled into incest.

The arrival of Information Minister Fraga Iribarne brought intelligence to the official scene, however, and the situation has improved radically. Censorship was greatly lightened, Soviet and East European films imported, and the most difficult work of the foreign new wave shown in ordinary commercial cinemas or the several Art Cinemas springing up since 1967, which offer original versions with subtitles. The State's Film School has produced a whole crop of lively young directors, and Spanish work at last wins international prizes, with names like Picazo and Summers, Regueiro and Patino tackling worthwhile themes and displaying skill and flair. Saura's Civil War symbol *La caza* is a supremely concentrated and effective study, worthy of the absent master of Spanish film-makers, the Aragonese (like Goya) Luis Bunuel. The main threat to good film production now lies in the purely commercial outlook of the powerful distributor and exhibitor organisations.

The way to the distributors' hearts is via co-production, which adds Italian star-anatomy to the cast while preserving the Spanish quota rights (1 to 4 ratio of Spanish production to foreign, though showing of Spanish films qualifying for the highest category of quality carries special dispensations). In a boom year like 1963, 62 of the 180 films shot in Spain were co-productions. Though output is high, not all of it reaches the screen. At the same time, Spanish sunshine and varied countryside draws countless foreign companies to make their films here on location, and thus Lawrence of Arabia gallops over the sand dunes of Almeria, and Dr Zhivago's Moscow is a film-set outside Madrid. There is even a complete Wild West township used in dozens of Spanish-Italian cowboy epics, the so-called ' spaghetti-Westerns.'

LITERATURE

The twentieth century has been a rich one in Spanish letters, starting with the Generation of '98—philosopher novelist Unamuno, essayist Azorin, poets Antonio Machado and Juan Ramon Jimenez (Nobel winner), as well as novelist Pio Baroja and the many-sided Valle-Inclan, whose *Ruedo Iberico* is one of the finest political-satiric novels in any language. The historian Menendez Pidal (who died in 1968 at the age of ninety-nine) linked this generation to the men of the 20s and 30s, thinkers Ortega y Gasset and Ramiro de Maeztu, novelist Perez de Ayala, historian Americo Castro and biographer-essayist Dr Marañon, as well as the brilliant Madariaga, whose *Spain* is an impressive guide to the nation, and whose *Ingleses, Franceses, Españoles* hits off these national characters to perfection.

Less accessible to the outside world, the surrealist Gomez de la Serna, satirist Fernandez Florez and essayist Julio Camba, all of this period, offer much delight to the reader. The left-wing poets of the Civil War include Garcia Lorca, Miguel Hernandez and Rafael Alberti, the latter surviving outside Spain. The virtues of the right wing do not seem to have produced anything of similar calibre, though Peman is a fine poet and versatile writer.

The tragedy of war and the almost as grim aftermath, hampered by censorship and clouded by hatreds and propaganda, did not help literature, and the eventual outcome was a ' tremendist ' or black school of novelists led by the half-English

Camilo Jose Cela. Several impressive women novelists have also made their mark, and the liberalisation introduced by Fraga Iribarne, especially with the 1966 Press and Printing Law, has made a vast difference to what Spaniards can read and write, even though the writers may well complain of the remaining hindrances to free speech. It depends on whether comparison is made with the situation in the rest of Europe or with the benighted political and religious censorship formerly prevailing in Spain.

Today the Civil War, treated with considerable objectivity as wounds heal, is the best-selling subject matter in Spain, though still a small percentage of the 12,000 or so titles published here annually, over half of them in Barcelona, brought out by 563 publishers throughout the country, and sold through 1,300 bookshops. Exports (£15, $36 million) mainly to South America are money-spinners, but the home market remains obstinately small. Some blame the high prices (18s, $2 to 50s, $6 for normal books) for the small sales (3,000 is good for a novel); others blame the small sales for the high prices. Other culprits are the myriad firms with antiquated machinery and the small readership because of insufficiently widespread secondary education. The high cost of Spanish paper also contributes.

Literature and arts subjects in general account for under half the total number of titles, with religion, social science and pure and applied science normally accounting for over a thousand apiece. A quarter of the number may be translations, with English language books easily first. But translators are even poorer than the writers themselves, playwright Alfonso Sastre receiving £42 ($100) for his six months translating all Sartre's drama. Save for the big prize-winners (Nadal, Planeta and others ranging from £600, $1,440 to £1,600, $3,840) sometimes criticised as merely receiving royalties in an advance lump sum to generate publicity, life for a Spanish author is a grim affair of ill-paid hack-work and journalism for survival, while creating more or less in his spare time.

PRESS

The press is the window on to a nation which cannot lie. For nearly a quarter of a century after the Civil War the Spanish press was merely an instrument of Government propaganda, material all vetted by the censor, instructions given as to what should be mentioned, on what page, in what size type and so forth, what should be attacked, what defended. Not surprisingly, Spain's readership for newsprint has been one of the world's lowest. The National Movement chain of papers naturally voiced the propaganda with enthusiasm, while the many other papers, right-wing but not Falangist, had to convey real information or opinion between the lines. The Spaniards who could not be bothered to read between lines turned instead to the underground network of political joke and rumour, infinitely more ribald and virulently damaging to official prestige than the truth in print would have been. No mention of strikes or troubles crept into this tomb-like press, and Spaniards could learn what was happening in their own country only via the foreign press, which would be withheld from sale in Spain if it contained over-strong reports. The result has been an inoculation of Spaniards against belief in official information.

However, a change came over the scene in 1962 with the new Information and Tourism Minister, Fraga Iribarne, and a notable liberalisation of communications media. He convinced the Government that a dead press was useless as an instrument, but even so, it was four years before he could fight through the Press Law eventually passed in April 1966 and fitted with several dozen snags and hindrances to restrain journalists and reassure the reluctant hawks in the Cabinet.

The Press Law limited editorships to journalists carrying the professional's card (obtained by study at one of three centres); laid out a series of vague principles and subjects which were untouchable (' truth ' as defined by the Government, the ' Principles of the National Movement ') on pain of confiscation of the offending issue by the courts or administrative sanctions by the Ministry of Information. As in baseball, editors offending thrice would be struck out. Issues still had to be deposited at the Ministry before distribution for last-minute inspection. Unspecified but no less real influences on the press were linked with newsprint supply and the official EFE news agency, handling foreign news.

In Spain's political context nothing more ambitious could have been obtained—or preserved. But the crucial difference was that instead of official censors consigning all inconvenient facts to silence and the waste-paper basket as formerly, they now had to challenge an item they objected to in the courts, which in practice almost invariably found in the newspapers' favour. The administrative fines (not controlled by the courts in the first instance) have produced some Kafkaesque harassment for outspoken magazines like Barcelona's *Destino*, Madrid's left-wing Christian Democrat *Cuadernos para el dialogo*, and *Gaceta universitaria*. At the same time, Church-sponsored worker and student reviews, formerly exempt from State censorship, have been squashed for their uncompromising words. But if the few have been given a rough time, the general press (over 100 dailies, mainly provincial) with 3 million circulation is at last able to report the reality of Spanish life.

The effect of the Press Law will in time be regarded as dramatic, second only to the commercial liberalisation of 1959 and the logical outcome of the pressures and modernisation then started. In a land which specialises in political non-events, these two measures were indeed events, ending stagnation but at the same time offering a safety valve to achieve progress without provoking explosion. To this extent, the hawks most dubious about these steps are unwittingly being aided. Reality demands change, but closes the alarming unacknowledged gap between Government and governed. Education, social security, labour organisation (the material gathered in this book was simply not available three years ago), factors in comparison with which more obviously ' political ' items are but superficialities, are brought under examination in the papers. Cortes Members speak out, knowing that at last they can be heard in the nation. Before this great change Spain could be assumed to enjoy everything—like the picador's horse—because its vocal chords were cut. Such ignorance was a true peril for the future.

As for the press itself, this is still heavily regionalised, which means small circulation for even the stronger Madrid and Barcelona press, whose most revered organs, *ABC* and *La Vanguardia*, run off 200,000 to 250,000 copies apiece each morning, a third to a half of the space taken up with advertising, the style respectable but stodgy, the news late, and most coverage via the daily *cronica* from correspondents abroad, events (if any) drowned in literary bechamel. *ABC* is Monarchist, Madrid *Ya* is right-wing Christian Democrat, the capital's livelier *Pueblo* is owned by the *Sindicatos* but its former rival *El Alcazar* is no longer independent, though its stable has given birth to *Nuevo Diario,* a morning paper with more news-sense and modern layout than the others. Pamplona's lone Carlist daily *El Pensamiento Navarro* is outspoken, and Spanish events are well covered by the excellent ' Time '-style weekly magazines *SP* and *Mundo.* The economy is abundantly served by magazines, and *La Actualidad Española, Gaceta Ilustrada* and *Triunfo* are big glossies with bite.

RADIO AND TELEVISION

Spain's crop of local radio stations have been pruned from their 500 or so of the early 60s, most of them tiny local transmitters. The pop music and advertisement stations are now grouped under the National Movement, Church and private chains, which carry the two main news bulletins of the State network, *Radio Nacional*; the latter, a department of the Information Ministry, carries no commercials. Its Madrid and regional stations offer varied if low-budget fare, and the second, educational channel is an occasional oasis of good music.

The two-thirty and ten o'clock news features have good, live foreign coverage, buried like plums in the semolina of official doings. 'The end of the world is scheduled for three-ten this afternoon, but first, our correspondent in Albacete reports on the inauguration of the new municipal fish-market,' would cause no surprise, were people by then actually listening. For the additional propaganda pieces, the readers adopt tones of reverent uplift, or Gothic scorn, as the case requires.

Like *Radio Nacional, Television Española* is also a Ministry agency, and a potent political weapon when the message is put over as saturation advertising, like the costly spots which finance TV and worry the non-State newspapers as a rival for advertising revenue. The sole television undertaking, *TVE* has a second, educational channel, and studios in Barcelona as well as the modern Prado del Rey installations outside Madrid. Much of the midday to midnight transmission material is composed of British and American serials (the latter dubbed into Mexican sibilance), but bullfights and football draw closest attention on three million or so sets all over the country. The drama features can be excellent, and the distance covered since the humble start in 1956 is shown by the Spanish features recently sweeping the international TV prize scene.

STATE AID

The State is always expected to do things Spaniards require but will do little to provide, and this applies also in the cultural sphere. Films are heavily subsidised, the worthy commercial product entitling its producer to an advance of 15 per cent of the first six years' gross, a million pesetas of this provided on completion. Work which promises to be of high artistic merit gets priority in application for official credit to finance it, and advantageous distribution and screening opportunities. This entire system has been brought out of the bureaucracy and into the world of reality, of critical and commercial success in recent years.

Film box-office taxation (now closely checked by the Ministry of Information and Tourism) helps subsidise the theatre, with small allowances for touring companies and support for the National Theatres. However, the most obvious example of State aid for the arts is the Festivals of Spain scheme, whereby light opera, drama and ballet companies of good quality tour every corner of Spain, together with art films, art and sculpture exhibitions and explanatory talks. For a cost of around £500,000 ($1,200,000), some sixty festivals, with combinations of ten times as many items, will tour in a single season. Plays by Ionesco, Spanish *zarzuelas*, abstract art, a foreign ballet company in the incredible Caves of Nerja—these are both a distraction for the tourist and a breath of culture for the Spanish provinces which could never hope to see such things brought commercially, for only a quarter of the expense comes back at the reasonably-priced box-office. Altogether a fine scheme, and one which incidentally provides welcome employment for numerous artists in the slack summer season.

Appendix

HINTS FOR VISITORS

WHEN

July and August are the peak tourism months, when Spain's generally low prices are at their highest, and generally high service at its lowest. Only advance booking can secure hotel accommodation on the coast resorts, while Madrid and Barcelona, though emptier, are too hot for comfort. The big cities can be at their crisp best in autumn or January, but international congresses tend to occupy the hotels. Spring is wet from March onwards.

MADRID

The businessman may have as much to do in Bilbao and Barcelona as in the capital, but Madrid has the best of everything to offer, restaurants, flamenco, shops, and sixteen bullfights during the May San Isidro festivities. The old town is attractive, and the new town new. The main draws are fascinating old towns within an easy morning's drive or coach tour—Toledo, El Escorial, Aranjuez, Segovia, all between twenty and forty miles away. For Madrid as for the other Spanish cities, a Foldex map (obtainable anywhere in Spain) is an essential companion.

MOTORISTS

Gasoline ranges from 85 octane to 96 octane 'super.' The international companies do not market gasoline in Spain, which is all provided by the Campsa monopoly. The difference is thus between Campsa gas at Campsa's occasional directly-owned stations, and 'baptised' or adulterated Campsa at too many of the private stations. Speed limits are not a problem, but beware infringing no overtaking signs, as the Civil Guard patrolmen are implacable. Always hoot when overtaking, or when reaching blind corners. Priority goes to the vehicle coming from the right if the roads are of equal importance, unless otherwise specified. In Madrid and Barcelona, ask at filling stations for a 'blue zone' parking disc for use in the central areas. Set the disc at the hour you park, and don't try to change it later, as the time will have been noted down by traffic wardens. Ill-parked foreign cars are towed away as ruthlessly as native ones, and take hours to recuperate. Stealing from cars is not an industry, as in Italy, but refrain from leaving valuable items in full view when you park. *All* red lights mean stop, even when you make a right-angle turn through a green set, and come upon a red set barring further progress.

The red Michelin guide is essential for those driving long distances and passing through many towns. The State-run Paradors and Albergues are immensely satisfying hotels along the main routes, with excellent meals and service and low prices, frequently in romantic and spectacular settings such as old castles. For the individual regions of Spain, the series of Firestone maps are hard to beat. The Ministry of Information and Tourism gives complete and detailed lists of hotels and camping sites in publications well worth purchase.

MONEY

Spanish prices have risen over the past decade to a point not

far short of some European levels. However, excellent hotel accommodation (Spain's hotels are nearly all modern), wines and
spirits, as well as cigarettes, are still absurdly reasonable. Food
has become more expensive, but like accommodation, is strictly
supervised by the Ministry of Information and Tourism. All
extras and service charges have been previously incorporated in
the plainly visible prices of rooms or dishes, and there are no
unpleasant surprises when the bill arrives. Every establishment
must produce a complaints book if requested.

TIPPING

Widespread but not costly. A couple of pesetas is sufficient
for nightwatchman, taxi-driver or cinema usher. In the case of
restaurants, ten per cent is perfectly adequate. Twenty-five peseta
coins are useful for hotel tipping on arrival.

Bibliography

Brenan, Gerald. *The Spanish Labyrinth*. Cambridge University Press, 1962

Carr, Raymond. *Spain 1808-1939*. Oxford University Press, 1966

de Madariaga, Salvador. *Spain, a Modern History*. Jonathan Cape, 1961

Thomas, Hugh. *The Spanish Civil War*. Penguin, 1965

Spain. Ministry of Information and Tourism, Madrid

Spain, Education and Development. Country Reports, the Mediterranean Regional Project, OECD, Paris, 1965

Castro, Americo. *Los españoles: como llegaron a serlo*. Taurus, Madrid, 1965

de Madariaga, Salvador. *Ingleses, Franceses, Españoles*. Editorial Sudamericana, Buenos Aires, 1958

Tamames, Ramon. *Introduccion a la economia española*. Alianza Editorial, Madrid, 1967

Vives, J. Vicens. *Historia de España y America*, Vol V. Barcelona 1961

Anuario estadistica, España 1968. Instituto Nacional de Estadistaca, Madrid, 1968

Informe sociologico sobre la situacion social de España. Fundacion FOESSA, Euramerica, Madrid, 1966

Index